FOOTBALL
FOR
WOMEN

FOOTBALL
FOR
WOMEN

A FAN'S GUIDE TO THE RULES, PLAYS AND STRATEGY OF FAVORITE AMERICA'S PASTIME

Donna Poole Foehr

THIRD EDITION

Cover by Tony Greco

Library of Congress Cataloging-in-Publication Data

Foehr, Donna.
Football for women.

Bibliography: p. 175.
Includes glossary.
1. Football. I. Title.
GV950.6.F63 1981   796.332   87-14886
ISBN 0-915765-82-9

PRINTED IN THE UNITED STATES OF AMERICA

To my mother and dad, two very special people.

Acknowledgments

I would like to thank the following individuals and organizations for their assistance in the writing of this book: Michael Anderson, Arizona State University, Roy Beal, Frank Beckmann, Bob Boylston, John Butash, Joe Bushofsky, Canadian Football League, Dale Conquest, Jerry Cvengros, Joe D'Angelo, Detroit Lions, Mike Earle, Kent Falb, Dan Foehr, Don Foehr, Steve Foehr, Wayne Fontes, Rick Forzano, Al Fracassa, Joe Gardi, Gene Goldberg, Dr. Voigt Hodgson, Steve Horton, John Iaboni, Dan Jaroshewich, Leigh Johnson, Bob Kefgen, Carl Lemle, Sam Madden, Annabelle McIlnay, Michigan High School Athletic Association, Jerry Miles, Jane Morrissey, David Moss, National Collegiate Athletic Association, National Federation of State High School Associations, National Football League, National Football League Players Association, National Operating Committee on Standards for Athletic Equipment, Official Sports Center, Tim Pendell, Doug Ploe, Lee Rauch, Barbara Saliba, Fred Sible, Spin-Mask, Inc., Roger Stanton, Russ Thomas, University of Michigan and WJR Radio, Detroit, Michigan.

Third Edition edited by Todd A. Pruzan.

Contents

Prologue

This book is mainly about professional football as played in the National Football League (NFL), with other levels of the game explained in separate chapters. To omit any one of them would be like leaving out an important ingredient in a recipe. Since the rules differ very little between high school, college, NFL and Canadian football, once you understand the fundamentals you can understand the game at any level.

I went to football games as a student at Ohio University and then later when my older son played in high school, but I knew only the basics. My interest really grew when the Detroit Lions moved to the Pontiac Silverdome and we bought season tickets. The Lions originated in Portsmouth, Ohio (my hometown), and my dad never missed a game. My interest in football must be either inherited or contagious because I've missed only one home game during the last 15 years.

Why would a woman write a book about football? Certainly not from personal experience as far as the actual playing. A couple of reasons prompted the idea. First of all, I am an avid fan. Secondly, many people watching football games don't have the foggiest notion of what is really happening on the field. When I have attended games with friends I observed that many of the women (and some of the men) didn't understand football. If these few didn't, what about all the other spectators in the stands? I contacted the Community House in Birmingham, Michigan, and taught football classes for women there for four years. The people I taught knew very little about the game and were eager to learn, but I had too much information for them to absorb in such a short time. So I thought a book would be the perfect solution, allowing people to learn as much as they wanted at their own pace. I was also curious about what happened off the field, especially about equipment, training, and recruiting, and thought others would be, too.

In order to include information in the book that would appeal to everyone, I took three people to a football game. One knew nothing about the sport—and I mean zilch. Thought a right guard was deodorant. The second knew some basics, but not why a player is called a "tight end." The third was a knowledgeable fan who understood the game, but wasn't sure who did the "dog" and who did the "stunt" and why.

It's not my intention to coerce you into liking football just because it's the "in" thing to watch and talk about all fall. I'm giving you the benefit, however, of all my material; so it's up to you to learn as much or as little as interests you. But I'll bet the more you learn and understand what's happening on the field, the more fun you'll have; and you'll see how the game can become addictive. And you know what? *You'll* be the one who can hardly wait from one game to the next. You will become an expert fan.

Introduction

"We interrupt this marriage to bring you the football season. . . ."

Let's face facts—the game of football is here to stay. Sportswriters call fall the "Autumn Madness" because of all the football. The season begins each year in July with the pro training camps and ends with the Pro Bowl game over six months later. In between are the college draft and the spring mini-camps. Every day during this time, newspapers, radio, and television cover the happenings in football. Why be bored and an outsider just because you don't understand the sport?

Men grow up playing football in one form or another, so understanding it comes naturally to them. Women, on the other hand, have not played the sport; so understanding it takes a little longer for them. Given the chance, however, they can become knowledgeable about the game and enjoy it just as much as men.

Too many of us believe the statement, "Women follow soap operas; men follow sports." Last summer I heard one of the network executives being interviewed, and he said his company was scheduling programs directed toward women on Monday nights, opposite the weekly NFL football games on another network. During Super Bowl week stores plan special sales for women and suggest they come shopping while the men watch The Game. An ad in our local paper read, "LADIES! Rather golf than watch football? Join our free golf clinics. Sundays 1-4 PM."

John Madden, former head coach of the Oakland (now Los Angeles) Raiders and presently a CBS commentator on Sunday NFL games, has written two very humorous books. In his second one, *One Knee Equals Two Feet*, he comments on how a football addict comes back to the living after a football season ends:

"In February, start your recovery. Don't worry about relationships. Just get the blood flowing. You've been in hibernation. Walk around a little. Swing your arms. Stretch. In March or April, you can take care of birthdays, Mother's Day and all that stuff. But remember: In July the NFL starts training camp. Then you have to start getting into shape to sit around for six or seven hours at a time again."

To be sure, this is written tongue-in-cheek, but you'd be amazed at how much truth there is to it. The label of "football widow" is more than a joke. Women are stereotyped as not liking football. In fact, they often are interested in the game, but every time they ask something about it they're told, "It's too complicated" or, "You wouldn't understand it anyway."

Women who haven't had a chance to involve themselves in the game maintain their indifference and don't give themselves a chance to like it. It's natural for us not to like something we don't understand. I didn't enjoy football nearly as much until I began learning more about the game.

The younger generation is more exposed to football. As a result, they are more interested and can be credited with trying to dispel the notion of the "football widow" and other preconceptions. They know being a sports fan is not limited to a particular sex or age. A former neighbor, a 42- year-old woman, clears her calendar every Sunday during the football season so she can watch the Detroit Lions. If they aren't being televised, she listens to them on the radio and watches another game on TV at the same time. That may sound extreme, but she liked sports and started watching football. The more she watched, the more she learned. And the more she learned, the more she enjoyed the game.

Let me impress you with some statistics. Polls have shown that football has displaced baseball as our national sport. Three out of four people said they were pro football fans. This figure doesn't even include fans of college or high school football. A 66-year attendance record was broken in October 1985, when more than

900,000 fans bought tickets for a weekend of fourteen NFL games.

To show you the real impact of football, the 1986 Super Bowl drew the largest audience ever for a televised program—fifty-three percent of our population. Forty-six percent of the U.S. homes with a television set watched the 1987 contest.

Are you in awe yet? Read on:

Football is big-time show business. Eight of television's most-watched programs are football games. The ten highest rated sporting events of all time are all Super Bowls. It's incredible how one game can draw so much attention. Is it any wonder advertising spots for the NFL championship carry the highest price tag? The 1987 game commanded $600,000 for a 30-second commercial. That's not peanuts.

Football is perfect for television. It's one of the few live shows left. It is well-timed. It has a plot and commercial breaks. There is change and continuity. It is dramatic. It has a dependable quality and actors that come and go. Does that sound familiar? Like a soap? Who could ask for more? A soap and sport—combined! And what about the split screen TV where a different game can be seen on each side? If that doesn't inspire you to join the crowd, nothing will.

It might have occurred to you to learn more about football simply because you see other people enjoying it. Maybe you have a special friend who loves watching the game, or know someone in high school or college who plays on a team. Maybe you're a little league parent.

It's been said that "boredom is a woman at a football game." Don't believe it. It need not be. Many females have learned about the game and become enthusiastic spectators. Two women in my football classes are perfect examples. One was older and had a limited knowledge of the game, but wanted to learn more. By the end of the course she had a file card on each Detroit Lion player and said how much more she enjoyed watching their games since she "knew" the players. The other was younger and handed me a note after the last class that read, "Just wanted to thank you for sharing your knowledge and enthusiasm for the game! I can't believe what a help (the course) has been. You've opened a whole new world for me!"

If they can do it, so can you. Let me tell you how easy it is. First, you must have the desire to learn. All the information in the world is wasted if you're not interested in the subject. If you'd really like to understand football, the requirements are simple: time to learn important facts and time to watch some games. That's not asking much.

It's all up to you. A detailed glossary is included at the end of this book. Refer to it when you don't understand a term. You are not alone. It takes a while to get used to football terminology.

1

What is Football?

Before we start on the basics of football, I'd like to give you some background of the sport so you'll know how it got to be what it is today. A semblance of the game can actually be traced back 2,000 years to ancient Greece, so football didn't just happen. It grew from a rough beginning of trials and errors to become the polished game it is today.

Whatever its origins, the modern versions of the sport began in Britain. Football developed from rugby, an English form of football in which the forward pass is not allowed and play is stopped only for penalties. At the beginning, American college teams used soccer rules—advancing a round ball by kicking it—until a Canadian team introduced rugby football to America in 1874. Two years later, five schools formed a rugby football league. The players wore no helmets or pads, and since early play allowed pulling and dragging the ball carrier, some players had shoulder and hip straps on their uniforms so they could be pulled by their teammates toward the opponent's goal.

The Americanization of Football

The Americanization of football started in 1880 with the introduction of the line of scrimmage, followed closely by shortening the field to 110 yards, narrowing it to 53-1/3 yards, and limiting the number of players per team on the field to eleven. The first pro game was in 1895, but professional football struggled both financially and for recognition over the next quarter century.

At the turn of the century, numerous injuries and deaths still resulted from mass formations and gang tackling, and many institutions discontinued football. Others pleaded for the sport to be either reformed or abolished from intercollegiate athletics. As a result, some schools met in 1905 to form a governing body, which became known as the National Collegiate Athletic Association (NCAA) in 1910, to make and change rules and to see they were followed by its members. Football became a more respectable sport instead of a contest of brutality.

Within the next six years some major changes occurred. The forward pass was legalized, the field goal became worth three points, the touchdown six and the length of the playing surface was reduced to its present 100 yards.

Pro Football

In 1920 professional football became organized, and still more changes came. The quarterback became the first man to receive the snap from center, and plays were invented as well as the signal system. Since then the techniques of playing have evolved through the contributions of thousands of coaches and players to the way the game is played today.

Football is like a chess game played by two teams whose coaches, the master players, stand on either side of the field and manipulate the players. It is a timed contest of inches and seconds between two teams of eleven players each. The game is played on a rectangular field of grass or grasslike material with an inflated oval-shaped ball that is moved toward a goal, through or around the opposing team's line, by running, passing or kicking. Every scoring procedure is worth a specified number of points. Each team tries to score points while keeping the opposing team from scoring, so the team with more points at the end of the game is the winner.

An Evolving Sport

In comparison to baseball, where the rules for high school, college or professional play are essentially the same, football has not reached the same degree of uniformity. Since it is a body contact sport and requires split-second teamwork, it is quicker, more vigorous and involves greater physical contact the higher the level of play. Likewise, the maneuvers and strategies become more complicated.

Still, it's a young sport and subject to changes as new tactics and ways of performing are found. Rule changes are made with one or more of three goals in mind: to increase the safety of the players, maintain a balance between the offense and defense, and ensure more enjoyment for the fans. I'll give you examples of some recent revisions.

Since the quarterback wears less—and lighter —equipment and is in a defenseless position both during and after releasing the ball, he is more vulnerable to injuries than other players. When he is obviously restrained by the defense, he is considered "in the grasp" and may not be tackled.

To keep a balance between the offense and defense, all players may now thrust their hands forward with extended arms to contact their opponents.

The NFL has a common-opponent format for setting up team schedules for the upcoming year. For example, fourth place teams in a division play at least 12 of the next season's 16 games against common opponents. This means these teams are better balanced and more exciting to watch. In a poll asking people to name their favorite NFL team to watch, a surprisingly large number said they didn't have one. They said they preferred an evenly matched game, regardless of who the two teams were.

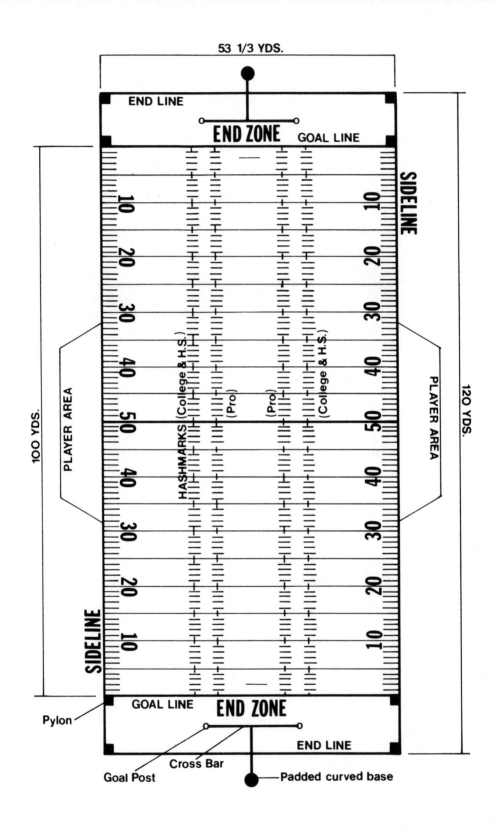

The Football Field

You know what a football field looks like, but what are all the lines called?

The football field is where all the action is. Besides being called "the field," the playing area is also known as "the gridiron" because the yard lines resemble the grids on a cooking utensil.

The Dimensions

You've heard the expression that it's "as big as a football field." A football field is 120 yards long and 53-1/3 yards wide (160 feet). The lines at each end are end lines and those on each side are the sidelines. Collectively, these lines are known as the boundary lines; the area of the field is measured inside these lines, and any action occurring on or beyond the boundary lines is out of bounds.

The playing surface—field of play—is 100 yards long and 53-1/3 yards wide (300 feet by 160 feet). It's bounded by goal lines and sidelines.

The End Zones

At each end of the field there is an end zone ten yards deep. It is bounded by the goal line, end line and sidelines.

The all-important goal lines that each team tries to cross to score points are eight inches wide, and separate the playing field from the end zones. All other lines are four inches wide.

There are eight pylons, flexible fluorescent markers, which are placed in the corners of the end zones. These markers help the officials determine whether or not a ball carrier is out of bounds.

The goal post is the bright, gold-colored metal structure offset behind the middle of each end line. It has an 18 foot, six inch horizontal crossbar directly above the end line. The crossbar is ten feet above the ground and connected by upright posts that extend 30 feet above the crossbar. The curved base of the goal post is padded to minimize injuries should players run into it.

Yard Markers and Hashmarks

The solid white lines from sideline to sideline are 5-yard markers called "stripes" or "yard lines." These five-yard lines extend four inches beyond the six-foot sideline border; they are used to assist the proper setting of the chains at the start of each series.

Large numbers indicate yard lines in multiples of ten, and they extend from goal line to goal line. They are numbered from midfield, which is the 50-yard line, to each goal line. These numbered lines indicate the distance to the nearer goal line. A white directional arrow is next to the top portion of each number (except the 50), and points toward the goal line in that half of the field.

Each of the 5-yard lines is marked with short perpendicular lines 70 feet, 9 inches in from each side. These are "inbound lines" or "hashmarks." In high school and college football the hashmarks are 53 feet, 4 inches from the sidelines.

Hashmarks are a very important part of the field. Whenever a play ends with the ball out of bounds (on or outside the sidelines) or between the hashmarks and the sidelines, the official brings the ball to the nearest in-bounds line and places it on the same yard line as the play just ended. If a play ends with the ball somewhere between these hashmarks, it remains there.

You may be wondering why hashmarks are used and why the ball isn't left where each play ends. The football must always be on the field of play before the start of each down; so when a play ends out of bounds, the ball must be brought back onto the field. By placing it on the hashmark, there is more room to run and pass the ball to either side of the field, rather than clogging the action near a side line. This means there are more possible plays and the game is more exciting for the fans.

There are short yard lines inside the sidelines and at the inbounds lines. They are at 1-yard intervals and enable the officials to measure exactly where the ball should be placed after a play ends and before the next one begins.

Two yards from the middle of each goal line, and parallel to it in the field of play, is a 1-yard-long solid line. This is where the ball is placed for a point-after touchdown try. In college and high school football, the PAT is from the three-yard line.

Coaching Area

The coaching areas are between the 32-yard lines, and all players who aren't actually in the game (except for one charting the game) must remain within this area. This is where the players watch the game when they are off the field.

The Basics

"The ball is spotted on the 50. As the two teams line up at the line of scrimmage—the defense in a 3-4 alignment and the offense in the wishbone formation—the rookie quarterback calls an audible. As the ball is snapped the pass rush is on, and the QB drops back in the pocket. He pump fakes and then pitches out to the fullback who picks up short yardage by swinging to the flat on the strong side."

Sound like a foreign language? Don't be alarmed. It's not gibberish, it's only football jargon. You'll see what I mean when you read an actual broadcast of a game in a later chapter. It isn't scary or hard to learn; the definitions are logical. After you learn the basics, read the chapters and become familiar with the terms, reread the paragraph. You'll know exactly what it means, and you'll be able to paint a mental picture of what's happening. It's that easy.

Understanding football language is the key to making the game a lot more fun to watch. I'm going to start you off with some very important points to learn first. You may already know some of these points, so it may be just a review.

Offense and Defense

The offense is the team in possession of the ball. This team tries to score points by advancing the ball toward the opponent's goal line by running, passing or kicking. It is moving away from its own goal line. Whenever you see or hear the word "offense," whether it's the "offensive line," a player like an "offensive back" or an "offensive formation," you'll know it's always the team with the ball.

The defense is the team without the ball. It defends the goal behind it by trying to tackle the offensive ball carrier, force him out of bounds or legally get possession of the ball before the offense scores. If "defense" is used in any way, like "defensive line," "defensive back," "defensive alignment" or "zone defense," you'll know it's the team trying to take possession of the ball.

Possession is Nine Tenths of Football

How does a team become the offense? When it *legally* gains possession of the ball. For instance, a defensive player cannot grab the ball away from the ball carrier after the official has blown the whistle to stop that play. However, the defense *can* get legal possession of the ball if:

- the ball carrier drops (**fumbles**) the ball in bounds while running or being tackled, and a defensive player either picks it up or falls on it before the whistle blows.
- a defensive player **intercepts** a pass (catches a thrown ball in bounds before it touches the ground) intended for an offensive receiver.
- the offense **doesn't move the ball** at least ten yards in four downs.
- a **punt** is securely caught.
- a **kickoff** is securely caught.
- a **field goal** attempt is unsuccessful.

Now you know how a team *becomes* the offense. What does it do when it *is* the offense?

Downs

The offense has four chances to move the ball ten yards toward the defensive team's goal line, and it gets to keep the ball (unless it scores) as long as it continues to advance it at least ten yards in these four tries. Each try is called a "down" or "play" and is the time that begins when the ball is first put into play (live ball), and ends when the ball is dead. I'll explain these in order—what a down is, how one begins and how one ends.

Understanding downs was one of the most difficult ideas for the students in my classes, so you may want to reread this section a few times. You'll get it.

In order for a team to earn a first down, it must advance the ball 10 yards, unless there's a penalty. (You'll learn about penalty yardage in Chapter 11. Once you understand downs, you'll have the foundation for learning how yardage assessed during penalties can affect downs.)

The first down is called "first and ten" (first down and ten yards to go for another first down). Suppose the offense moves the ball eight yards during the first down. The next down is then called "second and two" because there are only two yards to go for another first down.

What happens if the offensive team gains more than the two yards? Let's suppose it moves the ball five yards. This means the team has gained 13 yards in two downs (eight on the first and five on the second), earning itself a new first down because it advanced the ball more than the required ten yards. A team doesn't have to use four downs to gain ten yards. It can do it in one, two, three, or four plays, depending on how much yardage it has gained on each down.

You've just seen how a team can get a first down in two plays. Let's say that the offense moves the ball 11 yards on a first and ten, or maybe even 18 yards on the first down. No matter how many yards over the required ten are gained, the next down is still first and ten. The same reasoning applies if a team has a third and two and advances the ball five yards. The next down would still be first and ten because the offense has moved the ball at least ten yards in four *or fewer* downs.

Are you still with me? Hang in there—it gets easier.

Sometimes the offense isn't able to move the ball well. For example, it advances the ball three yards on the first down, two yards on the second down, and three more on the third down. That means the team has to advance two more yards on this fourth try, or forfeit the ball. (3 + 2 + 3 = 8; 10 yards are required for a first down.)

Near the Goal Line

Let me explain the terminology when the offense gets close to its opponent's goal line. If it has a first down within ten yards of the goal line, the term becomes "first and goal." It can't be "first and ten" because if the offense goes ten yards—or however many yards it actually is away from the goal line—it scores a touchdown and doesn't get another first down. So it's "first and goal" because the goal line is what the offense has to reach in four downs or give up the ball.

To Go

Now you know that "to go" means more than carry-out food. There is a short-hand way of explaining the down and the yards needed for a first down. You know the playing surface of the field is 100 yards long, with a 50-yard line dividing it into two equal sides. On each side of the 50 is a team's territory and the goal it is defending. So when you hear an announcer say "second and seven on the Dallas 34," it means it is second down with seven yards to go for a first down, and the ball is on the 34-yard line on Dallas' side of the 50-yard line. See how easy it is when it's broken down?

Measuring for First Downs

Unless there's a penalty when a down ends, the ball is placed (spotted) where the ball carrier's own forward progress was stopped. When it's difficult for the officials to tell by sight whether the ball was advanced enough for a first down, two assistant officials bring a 10-yard-long chain onto the field. The chain has a pole at each end. One end is placed at the point where the last first down was made, and the other is stretched toward the ball as it rests on the field. If the forward pole touches any part of the ball, it is a first down. Let's go on.

Live Ball (Game Action Starts)

After the referee signals that a new down can commence, a down begins when the ball is put into play. The ball then becomes a "live ball." This can be done in one of two ways—when it is snapped or when it is legally free-kicked to the opposing team.

When the player called a center "snaps" the ball, he releases it to the quarterback or to another teammate in a backward motion through his spread legs.

A free kick is one that puts the ball in play with a kickoff, safety kick, or fair catch kick (see Glossary). It's called a "free kick" because the opposing team must be at least ten yards away from the ball when it is kicked, and therefore, cannot interfere with it. In other words, the kicker is "free" from interference from the receiving team.

So, you've learned what a down is and how one begins. Let's see how one ends.

Dead Ball (Game Action Stops)

A down ends when the ball is whistled dead by an official. The most common times are when:

- a touchback occurs;
- the ball carrier or ball goes out of bounds;
- the ball carrier is tackled;
- a runner's forward progress is stopped;
- a forward pass hits the ground;
- a punted ball stops in bounds untouched by a member of the receiving team;
- a team scores points; and
- a field goal attempt is missed and ball is not run.

The time between a dead ball and its becoming live again allows the teams to regroup for the next down.

Blocking and Tackling

There are two other words you should learn now if you don't already know them: **block** and **tackle.**

"Blocking" is a term reserved mostly for the offensive team, because offensive players can't use their hands to knock down their opponents.

"Tackling" is a word associated with the defensive team, because defensive players can use their hands to pull down a player. They may not, however, hold an opponent.

If you learn what I've just given you in this chapter, you'll find the rest of the book to be easy to understand. Learning football is like putting a puzzle together. Once you start getting the pieces to fit, the puzzle gets easier. The more you learn, the easier the pieces fit together.

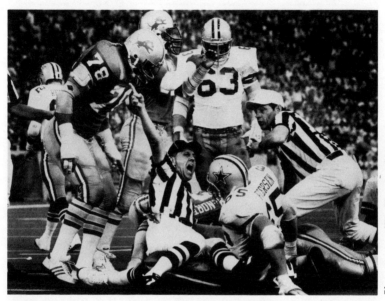

Officials occasionally get involved in the action too.

4

Scoring Fundamentals

The name of the game is earning more points than the other team when the game ends. How does a team get points? By scoring touchdowns, field goals, safeties and point-after touchdowns. Let's look at each one.

The Touchdown

We all know where the diamond ranks among jewels. Who doesn't? Well, the touchdown (TD) is the top prize in scoring. The most points a team can score in one play is six—a touchdown. This happens when the ball crosses or touches the opponent's goal line while legally in possession of a player who is in bounds. It is accomplished by:

- running into the end zone.
- passing the ball to an offensive player who catches it in the end zone.
- recovering a fumbled ball in the defenders' end zone.

We already know that an offensive team gets four chances to advance the ball ten yards. If it is successful in its attempts, the team continues until one of five things happens:

1. It scores a touchdown.

2. It loses the ball by a fumble or an intercepted pass.

Official showing signal for a touchdown, successful extra point or field goal.

3. It can't gain ten yards in four tries, so then must give up the ball to the opponents on the same yard line the previous play ended. This happens when the offense has a fourth down, generally short yardage (about a yard or two) to make a first down, tries it, and fails. There are two times in particular when a team usually decides to keep the ball on a fourth down. One is when it has good field position and thinks it can gain the necessary yardage for a first down. The other is when it is behind toward the end of the game, and must retain possession of the ball in order to have a chance at scoring. (This happened once in a Houston Oilers-Detroit Lions game. The Oilers were behind 24-13, and had a fourth down, with 1 yard to go for a first down, on the Lions' 6-yard line. Normally, a team would attempt a field goal to score three points, but there were only four minutes left in the game. Since Houston needed two touchdowns to win the game, they went for the first down. They didn't get it, so the Lions gained possession of the ball).

4. It punts. When the offense has used three downs, hasn't gained much yardage (or even lost some because of a quarterback sack or a penalty) and is too far from the goal post to try a field goal, it will usually relinquish possession of the ball by punting. This moves the receiving team farther from the kicking team's goal line. A player called a punter, whose specialty is punting, takes the kick. He stands about 15 yards behind the center, who hikes the ball directly to him. He then drops it and kicks it before it hits the ground. Even though the punter kicks the ball from a spot 10-15 yards behind the line, the distance is always measured from the scrimmage line.

5. It attempts a field goal.

The Field Goal

A field goal (FG) holds the second highest scoring value in football—three points. When the offensive team has a fourth down, does not think it can make a first down, and is within the placekicker's range, it tries a field goal. (A field goal cannot be scored on a punted ball.) This means a special player, the placekicker, comes onto the field. A teammate receives the centered ball approximately seven yards behind the line of scrimmage, and holds it upright, on the ground, while the placekicker attempts to kick it through the opposing team's goalposts. If the ball touches the crossbar or one of the posts and goes through, it is "good" and counts for three points.

How do they figure the distance for a field goal? Let me explain. The placekicker must kick the ball from the holder's position, seven yards back from the line of scrimmage, through the uprights of the goal post, ten yards beyond the goal line. In other words, every time you hear about a field goal attempt, add 17 yards to the distance from the line of scrimmage to the goal line, and you'll know how far the ball must be kicked for a successful field goal. If the kick is successful, the offensive team is awarded three points and then must kick off to the other team.

If the ball doesn't go between the uprights, the field goal attempt is unsuccessful. In this case, the defending team then has a choice. It can run the ball back towards the kicking team (which rarely happens because the ball usually goes into the end zone) or it can let the ball be whistled dead. If the ball is blown dead, the official puts the ball either on the same line it was snapped from during the field goal attempt, or on the 20-yard line, whichever is farther from the new offense's goal line (they were the defense before the ball was kicked).

For example, if a team tries a field goal from the 15-yard line and misses, the ball would be put on the 20-yard line because the 20 is five yards farther from the new offense's goal line. If the same team tried a field goal from the 35-yard line and missed, the ball would be placed on the 35-yard line because it is 15 yards further away from the new offense's goal line than the 20-yard line. This rule keeps teams from trying field goals from just anywhere on the field.

Let me give you an example of how this rule affects strategy on the field. Suppose a team is trying a field goal from the 50-yard line. That would be a 67-yard attempt. The longest field goal, 63 yards by Tom Dempsey, was scored in 1970. Someday the record will be broken, but for now it stands, so a team would think twice about trying a field goal from the 50-yard line. But suppose a coach wants it tried anyway. If the kicker misses, the new offensive team can either run the ball back or get possession of the ball on the 50-yard line. That's halfway to the opponent's goal line and a team usually wouldn't want to give up the ball at mid-field—so they would normally punt instead.

Before we go on, let's review what happens when a team gets possession of the ball:

1. It continues advancing the ball at least ten yards in four downs until it scores a touchdown;

2. It loses the ball by fumbling or having a pass intercepted;

3. It cannot gain ten yards in four attempts so it loses possession of the ball "on downs";

4. It punts; or

5. It attempts a field goal.

We've already looked at touchdowns and field goals. Let's move on to the third method of putting points on the scoreboard.

The Safety

A safety (S) is the only way a defensive team can score points without taking possession of the ball. Two points are awarded to the defense if:

• the offensive ball carrier is tackled behind his own goal line, provided he wasn't pushed or dragged there by the defense.
• a blocked punt goes out of the kicking team's end zone.
• a receiving team's player touches or acciden-

tally kicks the punted ball while trying to pick it up, and forces it into his own end zone where he or a teammate recovers it.

● the offensive team commits a foul in its own end zone and the penalty would be enforced from the spot of the foul.

Official signal for a safety.

Not only is the defensive team given two points for a safety, but the offense must also give up the ball by kicking off from its own 20-yard line. The safety kick differs from a regular kick because it can be made either by place kick, drop kick or punt. A kicking tee may not be used. This is the only time a team that scores the points receives the kickoff. Normally, a team kicks off from the 35-yard line, so you can see how the receiving team has a definite advantage after scoring a safety.

This is a good time to mention intentional safeties that teams sometimes give up. Suppose it's close to the end of a game, and the offensive team is ahead by three points with the ball deep in its own territory. If it loses the ball, the other team could easily score either a field goal to tie, or a touchdown to put them ahead by three points. So it chooses to have the ball carrier step back into the end zone, down the ball, and give up two points. It's still ahead by one point. True, it must kick off to the other team, but the kick would probably put the ball on the other side of the 50-yard line and make it more difficult for the other team to score before the game ends. It's a gamble, but one that is probably worth it.

Planning is one thing. Executing those plans is another. That's one of the things that makes football so exciting—22 players carrying out 22 different assignments. Anything can happen.

The Point-after Touchdown (PAT)

One point is scored after a touchdown by placekicking the ball through the uprights. When a team scores a touchdown, the clock is stopped, the ball is put on the specially marked 2-yard line and the scoring team is given one more down to score an extra point. In other words, it is a chance for a bonus. The ball is centered to a teammate, who holds it upright on the ground for the placekicker at the 10-yard line. Since the uprights are ten yards beyond the goal line, the PAT is a 20-yard kick. It usually seems like a sure bet, but some are missed or blocked.

The extra point may also be scored by successfully running or passing the ball over the goal line. This method can be used when there's a bad snap from center and the holder, usually a quarterback, can't get the ball down quickly enough for the kicker. Whether or not the point-after touchdown is successful, the kicking team must give up possession of the ball by kicking off.

The Two-point Conversion

The two-point conversion after a touchdown occurs only in high school, college and Canadian football. The teams line up the same way they would for a one-point try (high schools and colleges on the 3-yard line and CFL on the 5-yard line), but instead of kicking the ball, the offense tries to cross the opponent's goal line by running or completing a pass. Why isn't the two-point conversion used all the time? Because the defense lines up at the line of scrimmage with anywhere from six to eleven men, making it difficult for the offense to get across the line at all. With the one-point placekick, the holder is back several yards, and this gives the kicker more time to get the ball airborne.

Let's see what happens with extra-point tries in high school, college and Canadian football. Suppose a team is behind 14-7 in a game and scores a touchdown. If it tries the one-point kick and succeeds, the score is tied 14-14, but if it goes for the two-point conversion and is successful, it would be ahead 15-14. Which would you go for?

It would be logical to go for the two-pointer, but it really isn't all that simple. If the team goes for the two points and misses, it would be behind 13-14, and there may not be time enough to score again before the game ends. That's why a coach is a hero if his decision works and a goat if it fails, even though he had nothing to do with the execution of the play.

The two-point **defensive** conversion is a college and CFL rule. On a PAT, the defense can advance a fumble—in college games, if the defense is on or beyond the line of scrimmage, and anytime in the CFL—or block the kick, intercept the pass and advance the ball to the opposite end zone for a two-point safety.

In the CFL, both one- and two-point offensive conversions after touchdowns are called "converts," and it is possible to score a one-point play called a "single" or "rouge." See Chapter 20 for a more complete description of Canadian football.

Summary of Scoring

Below is a list of the methods of putting points on the scoreboard:

Touchdown (TD)—6 points

Field Goal (FG)—3 points

Safety (S)—2points

Point After Touchdown (PAT)—1

Two-point Conversion—2 points (high school, college and CFL)

Two-point Defensive Conversion—2 points (college and CFL)

5

The Players

People often complain about professional athletes because of their high salaries and threats of strikes. Imagine going to the theater with a beautiful stage setting and an orchestra playing, but no actors. Or sitting down with a friend at a chess board with no chessmen. You can have everything necessary for a football game—field, officials and equipment—but without players, you have nothing.

Sometimes fans say certain players aren't good enough to play in the NFL. But let me tell you just how difficult it is to "make it" in professional football.

There are roughly 15,000 high school, 650 college and 28 NFL teams. College teams carry as many players as their conference allows; one team has 138 on its roster. Presently, the NFL limit is 45 active and two inactive players. Even though all collegiate players are not seniors or otherwise eligible for the draft, you can see the odds of becoming a professional football player are not encouraging. Those who do make it are the cream of the crop.

The average American pro football player's career in the NFL lasts 3.6 years. Some play much longer, however. Tony Dorsett and Walter Payton both retired after playing 13 seasons.

The Two Platoon System

Players used to play both offense and defense, but we have reached the age of specialization. Now they play either one or the other. This "two platoon" system allows teams to substitute players without limits at any time except when the ball is in play. It lets the players focus their attention and talents on the part of the game they excel in, and since one platoon is resting while the other is on the field, the fresh unit can compete at full speed when it's called upon. The players who play most of the time with their unit are the "first string." The choice replacements are the "second string" and the next, the "third string."

You're probably wondering how each team gets its allotment of players. There are several ways: college draft, free agents and Plan B free agents, trades and try-out camps. I'll tell you about each one of them.

The College Draft

Scouting college players for the NFL draft is well-organized. There are two talent groups, National Scouting and BLESTO (Bears, Lions, Eagles and Steelers Talent Organization), that rate the collegiates. Pro teams combine and split the cost to pay for the service. Twenty-one of them use National and seven use BLESTO.

The two groups begin work on the next year's seniors immediately after the spring draft, using a great deal of research. Though 15,000 college seniors play football, maybe one- tenth of them are actually rated for possible pro material.

Team scouts look at regular and post season game tapes and visit many colleges during the year. BLESTO and National combine their lists of prime potentials and invite about 350 seniors to a three-day "physical week" with NFL coaches. The players undergo evaluation where they are examined, tested, timed, probed, X- rayed and interviewed. This annual event gives the coaching staff an opportunity to see which players will most likely fit in and represent the image the pro team wants. Since there are only 336 players (28 teams and 12 rounds) chosen in the annual draft, teams have the luxury of being selective. Before the draft each team makes a list of the players it wants and the order of preference. Quite often the head coach personally visits several prospects.

Until recently, it had been the policy of the NFL not to draft a player before he completed four seasons of college eligibility, had been in college for five years or had earned a degree; now, younger college students are also drafted. The NFL never drafts players directly out of high school.

The draft takes place the last week in April in New York City, with representatives from all teams. Each team designates a person to announce its selections. The pro team finishing last in the standings the previous season gets the first pick in the first round of the draft, the second-to-last gets the second, and so on until the team with the best record gets the 28th choice.

This is the first round and any player chosen in this round is called a "first round draft choice." The second round follows the same procedure, as do the later rounds until the last round, which now is the twelfth.

If you're wondering why it's done this way, it's to create parity in the league. If the teams with the poorest records get to choose at the beginning of the draft, it is hoped that all the teams will become evenly matched. The theory is good, but other factors such as injuries, free agents and roster trades keep teams balanced. Many drafted college players don't "make it" in the NFL. Supremacy, therefore, changes over time.

Every team doesn't go after the same player. For example, suppose the top player on the scouting list is a quarterback and the teams with the poorest NFL records don't need quarterbacks. They'll pick whatever player they want, like a running back or a defensive tackle, so the quarterback is still available to the next team in order. A team can buy, sell, or trade any of its places in the present or future draft to any other team.

After the draft, teams begin salary negotiations with each player and/or his agent. A player must have a signed contract before he can practice and play with the team. Do you have any idea what a player receives for signing a contract to play football in the NFL?

Base salaries for roster players presently range from $50,000 to $2.5 million annually. The average salary in 1989 was $300,000. About one percent of the players have contracts guaranteeing a specific annual salary, while the others are paid per game. New players are paid bonuses for signing, reporting to training camp and making the team. They, and some veterans, receive personal endorsements and deferred compensation, such as annuities and/or real estate. Performance incentives are also written into most contracts, rewarding players if they throw or catch a specific number of touchdown passes, gain exceptional yardage or sack quarterbacks.

Most teams conduct a spring mini-camp—usually for about three days—shortly after the draft to see how the rookies stack up with the veterans and free agents who were signed. It's also a time to assess injuries of the veterans and see who will be invited to summer camp from the 90 or so players attending.

A supplemental draft may be held in June for college players who have become eligible to play for reasons like early graduation. The procedure for selecting these players differs from the regular draft in that the names of each of the 28 teams are put into a drum and a draw determines the order in which they will choose the players. The number of chances to get a low pick is based on a team's win/loss record the previous season, with the worst team getting 28 chances and the best, one. Whatever pick a team uses in this draft will be deducted in the regular draft the next year. For example, if a team selects a player in the second round of a supplemental draft, it forfeits its second round choice in the next regular draft.

In July the new players go to the pre-season summer training camp of the franchise that chose them. They are not automatically on the team. They must qualify by proving themselves capable of playing professional football. Even after all this, only about one-half of those drafted actually "make it!" Just to show you how difficult it is to make an NFL lineup: of the 336 rookies chosen in the 1987 draft, about half made their team, but only 29 were starters.

Free Agents and Plan B Free Agents

A free agent is free to negotiate and sign with any team. He can be a college player who was not drafted or a professional player not under contract with any team.

Plan B allows teams to protect 37 of their players, leaving the rest free to sign with any other teams between February 1 and April 1.

Trades

Unrestricted trading of player contracts/rights is allowed through mid-season and then ends until February, so there is a relatively small amount of trading signed players after the season begins.

Try-out Camps

Some pro teams conduct try-out camps to find potential players not previously scouted, but most teams require a letter or phone call before granting a try-out.

A team may release a player at any time—unless he is injured—and usually does so by placing him on waivers. This means any of the other 27 teams has 24 hours to claim him by paying the same salary as the team releasing him. If no team claims him, he is unconditionally released with no team financial obligations (unless he has a guaranteed contract). He is now a free agent. However, if he has played in the league at least four years, he is vested and will receive guaranteed payments (no more than eight games' salary) if he is cut between the first and eighth games.

An injured roster player is different. He cannot be cut from a team while on the injured reserve list and will continue to receive his per-game pay during the season of injury only—not for any subsequent period.

Offense: The Ticket-Sellers

It's been said the offense attracts the crowds and sells the tickets.

There are so many blocks, running plays, passes and passing routes that it's incredible to think a person could learn them all. Luckily, we don't have to. We're not the players.

The job of the offense is to move the ball toward the opposing team's goal line. The functions of the different players vary according to whether they are on the line or in the backfield, whether they are a tight end or a wide receiver.

Some players' positions are defined as "left" or "right," referring to the side of the ball where they line up prior to the start of a down.

The Offensive Line

A team is only as good as its offensive line. No matter how skilled the running back or the quarterback—if his offensive line does not block effectively, he will have difficulty moving the ball. The middle five players on the offensive team's line of scrimmage are the **left tackle** (LT), **left guard** (LG), **center** (C), **right guard** (RG) and **right tackle** (RT). They make up the **interior line** and are called "interior linemen." When you hear an announcer say the battle is being fought in the "trenches," or the "pits," it's right here where the interior line meets the defensive line.

The Interior Line

The offensive linemen may block by thrusting their hands forward with extended arms, but they're not permitted to use their hands to hold. If a player is caught holding an opponent with his arms or hands, the penalty is ten yards for **offensive holding.** He also cannot push a defender while running interference for a ball carrier, or his team will receive a ten yard penalty for **illegal use of hands.** The interior linemen must be set (stationary) in a three-point stance for one second before the ball is snapped. This means they put one hand on the ground and crouch low to give themselves increased power when charging forward as soon as the ball is centered. If one breaks his three-point stance or pretends the start of a down *before* the ball is centered, the team is penalized five yards for **false start.** If any part of one of these players is in any way beyond his team's line of scrimmage when the ball is hiked, there is a five yard **offside** penalty.

The two jobs of the interior linemen are to block the defensive rush to protect the quarterback on passing plays, and to make holes and run interference for the ball carrier on running plays. The tackles are usually bigger and stronger than the other team players while the guards are quicker. If it's a pass, they'll step back after the snap to protect the quarterback. They cannot go more than one yard downfield from the line of scrimmage before the ball is thrown, or the team will incur a ten yard penalty for **ineligible man downfield.** If it's a running play, they move forward quickly to make a hole in the defense for the runner. Watch the offensive line in a game and you'll be able to tell at the snap what the intended play is by the movement of the interior linemen.

We've looked at the five interior linemen collectively,

but they have individual duties as well. The center has two responsibities. His main responsibility is to center the ball to the quarterback on running and passing plays, the holder on field goal attempts and point-after touchdowns or the punter. He lines up in a three-point stance, leans over the ball, and grasps it so the laces are to his left (if the quarterback is right-handed). As the quarterback calls the signal, the center hands the ball through his legs in a 1/4 turn so the ball ends up parallel to the scrimmage line. By doing it this way, he puts it in the quarterback's hands all ready for release and saves precious seconds.

When the center hikes to a punter or holder, however, he most likely uses two hands to control the ball better and get more distance. Unlike the quarterback, who is usually immediately behind the center, the punter stands 15 yards behind the line of scrimmage and the holder stands seven yards back. Instead of merely handing the ball back, then, the center must really throw it back between his legs when hiking to the punter or the holder. In this type of release, the ball goes rapidly through the air, perpendicular to the line of scrimmage. Since the two movements are different, some teams use a different center for each one.

A center's second job after snapping the ball is to block like the other four interior linemen.

It's important to know a tackle from a guard, because when you hear about a play off left tackle or a run around the right guard, you'll want to know where the runner went. One way of remembering where the linemen play is alphabetical. Start inside out with the center, guard, tackle—CGT. Another way is to think of the players on either side of the center as his body**guards.** That leaves only the tackles on the outside.

Odds and Ends

There must be seven men on the offensive line when the ball is snapped, or the team will be penalized five yards for **illegal formation** or **illegal procedure.** You've already learned about five players, so we need to look at the other two, known as "ends" because they line up at each end of the line. What do they do? Of the five players on the offense who are eligible to catch passes, two are the two endmost men on the line. One is called a **"tight end"** and the other a **"split end."**

The **tight end** (TE) lines up next (tight) to one of the tackles. He is the strongest of all the receivers because, besides being eligible to catch a pass, he can block on running plays just like the interior linemen. The side of the ball he lines up on, whether the left or right, is considered the "strong" side of the line because his presence makes one more shoulder-to-shoulder player on that side of the ball.

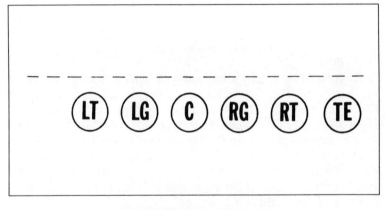

Diagram showing tight end

Split Ends

Split ends have nothing to do with your hair; they are receivers **split** several yards from the interior linemen.

The **split end** (SE), also called a wide receiver (WR), can also block, but his primary function is to catch passes. Since he lines up several yards away from the tackle, there is an open space on the line. Consequently, this side is known as the "weak" side of the line.

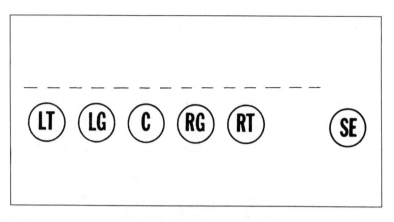

Diagram showing split end

As you look at the diagram you can see why the tight end's side of the line is strong. There's no space between the tight end and the tackle. On the split end side, there *is* an open area between the split end and tackle, so this side is more vulnerable to the defensive rush.

Depending on the formation and the kind of running or passing play, ends can be used in any combination—one tight end and one split end, two tight ends and no split end, or no tight end and two split ends—just so long as there are two. There could be more, but only the endmost two are eligible to catch passes.

We said another name for a split end is a "wide receiver." They get their name because they are the players used primarily for catching passes—**receiving** the ball—and they line up away—**wide**—from the interior line on or behind the line of scrimmage. They must be able to get down the field quickly and be able to catch passes. They have to get free from defenders with sharp and precise moves, hold on to the ball, and keep going for additional yardage. Some line up in a four- point stance (both hands on the ground) to take off like a sprinter, but most stand almost upright in a two-point stance. This stand-up position lets them check the defense as soon as the play begins. They usually cannot hear the quarterback's signal, so they must watch the ball very carefully.

The Quarterback

Now we come to the quarterback (QB), who is the offensive man in charge. He is the primary ball handler and passer. He must make things happen by throwing the right pass at the right time and scramble for a first down. There are certain requirements he needs to have in order to move the team down the field successfully. He must be smart enough to read defenses, catch blitzes and call the right audibles; he must have a strong arm and the ability to time the pass patterns and get rid of the ball quickly and accurately; and he must also be able to handle pressure.

The quarterback usually lines up immediately behind the center, though he stands five yards behind the center in the shotgun formation. The plays are usually decided by the coach and/or offensive co-ordinator, and it is the quarterback's job to make sure all the offensive players understand the routine of the upcoming play. They know he can change the play at the line of scrimmage, so they have to be alert. The quarterback calls the signal and receives the snap that starts every offensive down except kicking plays.

The Backfield

Besides the seven men on the line and the quarterback, three backfield men make up the 11-player offensive team. The backfield can be comprised of three wide receivers, two wide receivers and one running back, one wide receiver and two running backs or three running backs, depending on the formation. A **flanker** (FL) is a wide receiver who is a member of the backfield because he lines up at least one yard back of the line. He usually lines up on the same side as the tight end, about eight yards off to the side, but can line up on the split-end side or with the running backs. You already know about the wide receivers, so let's talk about running backs.

As the name implies, these players line up back of the line of scrimmage and are used mostly on running plays. Technically, they can line up anywhere as long as they are at least one yard behind the line, but they usually line up behind the quarterback. Collectively, they are called **running backs** (RB), but are categorized according to their position in the formation as **setbacks** (SB), **halfbacks** (HB), **fullbacks** (FB), **tailbacks** (TB), **slotbacks** (S) and **wingbacks** (WB). Besides running plays, they are used for short distance passes like the "screen" or "flare." They have farther to travel than a wide receiver when they get the ball, so they need speed and the instinct to see holes opening up.

Generally, a fullback is the largest and strongest because, besides being a runner, he is also a blocker, while the halfback has more running speed and is in on some pass plays. A setback is the lone back in the "One Back" formation while a tailback's position in the "I" and "Power I" sets is the farthest back from the line of scrimmage. A slotback lines up in the area (slot) between the split end and tackle, a yard behind the line of scrimmage in the "One Back" formation. A wingback's position in the "Wing" set is just to the outside of a tight end, and naturally, at least one yard behind the scrimmage line. (See **Formations**, Chapter 9.)

Summary

In this chapter you've learned about each of the 11 players on the offensive team. There must be seven players on the line of scrimmage. Five of them are the interior linemen: two tackles, two guards and a center. Two are ends, either split or tight, in any combination. They are eligible receivers.

The quarterback usually lines up immediately behind the center. There are three backs who may be wide receivers, or running backs. All of the backs are eligible to catch passes, as is the quarterback when he's in the shotgun formation.

Defensive Linemen

Linebackers

Defensive Backfield

7

Defense: The Game-Winners

The offense may sell the tickets, but it's a well-known fact that the defense often wins the games.

The defense has three basic positions: defensive linemen, linebackers and defensive backs. Let's start on the line with the defensive linemen.

Hold that Line!

You've heard the cheer, either in high school or college: "Hold that line!" It's a cheer directed at the linemen, or the defensive players on the line of scrimmage.

There can be any number of defensive players on the line, but usually it's three or four. Sometimes, in a **goal line stand** all eleven are on the line.

Linemen take a position opposite the offensive interior linemen in a three or four-point stance. Just as their names indicate, the ends line up on the outside.

If four linemen are used in a defensive alignment, they are **left end** (LE), **left tackle** (LT), **right tackle** (RT) and **right end** (RE). This is called an even defense. If an odd number of linemen make up the defenseive alignment, it's an odd defense—two ends and a middle player. The middle player has three names: **nose guard** (NG), **middle guard** (MG), or **nose tackle** (NT). He goes nose-to-nose with the offensive center. The defensive linemen are also known as the **"down linemen"**. Their jobs are to rush the quarterback on passing plays and to tackle the ball carrier before he cuts through the line on running plays.

Linebackers

The next group is called the **linebackers** because these players back up the defensive linemen by lining up just behind or alongside them. There can be any number, but usually it's three or four. If there are three, they are called left linebacker (LLB), middle linebacker (MLB) and right linebacker (RLB).

The middle linebacker is usually the defensive captain because he has the best view of the way the offense is lining up. The defensive coordinator, who is an assistant coach, usually determines the alignments.

If there are four linebackers, they are referred to as left outside linebacker (LOLB), left inside linebacker (LILB), right inside linebacker (RILB), and right outside linebacker (ROLB). The "left" or "right" is determined by facing the line of scrimmage, and "inside" and "outside" simply refer to the position of one linebacker in relation to the others.

Linebackers stand almost upright (two-point stance) or in a semi-crouch. They are the most versatile of the defensive players and their responsibilities are to defend against running plays and short passes. Some linebackers are used on special teams to block punts, field goal attempts, and extra- point kicks after a touchdown.

The Defensive Backfield

The last of the basic defensive positions is the backfield. Defensive backs can line up anywhere, but most of the time they line up behind the linebackers. They are known as the **"secondary."** The usual number is four, but like down linemen and linebackers, there can be any number of backfield players. The nickel defense, for example, involves five backfield players; the dime defense utilizes six.

Normally there are two **cornerbacks**, left (LCB) and right (RCB), and their positions are closest to the sidelines. The two **safeties, free** (FS) and **strong** (SS), play in between. The strong safety plays on the same side of the ball as the offensive tight end (TE).

Remember how the presence of the tight end gives the "strong" side of the line of scrimmage its name? That's

how the "strong safety" got his name—from playing opposite the offensive strong side of the line. The free
safety or "rover" plays on the weak side or is "free" to
roam. The secondary is supposed to defend against the
pass, especially a long one, and is the last line of defense
against a runner. These are the fastest players on the
defense.

When the safeties play man-to-man defense, each is
responsible for a particular offensive player. In a zone
defense, each player covers a specific area. (The area
where two zones overlap is called the "**seam**.") Occasionally, one or both of the safeties will "**blitz**" the quarterback—rushing him as soon as the ball is snapped.

Reacting to the Offense

The defensive team doesn't know exactly what the
offense is going to do or when the ball will be centered,
but it looks for clues. It watches for substitutions of
players, offensive formations, and any added pressure the
center might put on the ball just prior to the snap.
Defensive players can use their hands to push a blocker
out of the way, but they can't legally hold an opponent
other than the ball carrier or a player pretending to be
the ball carrier. If they do, they'll be penalized five yards
for **defensive holding**, and the offense will get an
automatic first down. They have no restrictions in lining
up, and can move before and during the snap, as long as
they don't draw an opponent offside or make contact
with an opponent *before* the snap—"**encroachment**"—or
have any part of their body across the line of scrimmage
during the snap—"**offside**."

Special Teams: Unsung Heroes

If the offense sells tickets and the defense wins games, what do the special teams do?

Special teams are truly the the unsung heroes of football. These are the players who come into the game for single assignments involving the kicking game. A few play on the first team, but most are second and third-string players and rookies (first year pros). They're as important as the offense and defense because one third of a team's total points are made by the kicking team. These players are used for and against kickoffs, punts, field goals and point-after touchdowns, but the same players are not used in every kicking play. In other words, "special teams" is not a single unit—there are several. Some players go in on return kick situations, others on offensive kicking. Certain kicks use a combination; for instance, strong blockers are necessary to attempt field goals, while tall players are needed to block field goal attempts. Speed is needed in getting downfield both on kickoffs and punts.

Kickers

We know a special teams squad is used on every kicking play, but who does the kicking? There are two specialists: the punter and the placekicker. What's the difference?

Some plays require the ball to be kicked after it has been released from the hands, but before it touches the ground. This is a punt and is used when a team voluntarily gives up possession of the ball during the game or following a safety (see Chapter Four for the safety kick). Other plays call for the ball to be kicked from a position on or near the ground. This is a place kick. The ball can rest on a plastic tee that holds it upright, as for a kickoff, or it can be held on the ground by a teammate, as for a field goal attempt or point-after touchdown. Since a punt is not allowed on the kickoff to start the game or second half, a placekick is used. It would be a logical choice anyway, because the ball can travel farther due to the lower trajectory.

Even though the use of each kick is clearly defined, there are situations when a coach must decide which one to use. For example, several factors are considered when deciding whether to punt or try a field goal:

- **Field position.** If the opponent's goal line is within range of the placekicker, it tries for a field goal. Otherwise, a team will usually punt.
- **Weather conditions.** If the field goal range is risky, but there's a strong wind against the opponent, a team probably try a field goal. However, if the wind is in its face, a team would be likely to punt because the wind holds the ball up.

- **Score.** If the score is close and field position is so-so, a team in the lead might punt because of the chance of missing a field goal attempt and giving better field position to the new offense. If the team is behind in the same situation, it would probably attempt a field goal to try to get some points on the scoreboard and cut the lead.

- **Competency of the Specialist.** If the placekicker had never kicked a field goal from further than 43 yards away, it isn't likely a coach would call for a 50-yard attempt; he would send in the punting team.

Punters and placekickers are very important to the team, and if a player is injured he will quickly be put on the injured reserve list and replaced, at least temporarily. If a player is not producing results as the coach expects, he will likely be put on waivers and removed in favor of a replacement, often a free agent. There is seldom the luxury of back-up kicking specialists on a roster, as in the offensive and defensive teams, so it's imperative they're at peak performance.

The Punter (P)

Suppose a team on the fourth down doesn't think it can make a first down and is out of range for a field goal. The punter is called to duty for either a "straight away" punt, "pooch," or punt into a "coffin corner." He stands about 15 yards behind the line of scrimmage, and the center snaps the ball directly to him. He makes sure the football's laces are up (the ball might deflect off to the side if his foot makes contact with the laces), takes a couple of stutter steps, and then kicks the ball from the top of his foot as quickly as possible.

Photo courtesy of Tom Albert/Detroit Lions.

If the ball is blocked by a defensive player *behind* the line of scrimmage, it is a loose ball and any member of either team may recover and advance it. If a member of the punting team recovers a blocked punt *beyond* the line of scrimmage, he cannot advance and the ball belongs to the receiving team.

A member of the punting team may not recover an *unblocked* punt that travels beyond the line of scrimmage unless the ball has first touched an opponent. This differs from the kickoff, where the ball has to travel only ten yards and then may be recovered by the kicking team.

If it's a long way downfield to the opposing goal line and he's doing a "straight away" punt, the punter kicks it as far and as high as possible, hoping for a good "hang time"—the time in which a kicked ball rises and descends—of between four and five seconds. A long hang time is important because it gives teammates time to get downfield before the ball comes down, keeping the receiver from gaining yardage after he makes the catch—or better yet, causing him to fumble the ball.

If the kicking team is near midfield, a coach may ask for a "pooch" or "coffin corner" punt. In a "pooch" punt, the punter kicks the ball very high and with enough backspin for it to come down and stop almost immediately—hopefully inside the defenders' 5-yard line. In a "coffin corner" punt, the punter aims toward one of the corners where the sideline meets the goal line. If done properly, the ball goes out of bounds along the sidelines and as close to the goal line as possible without going over it. When a ball goes out of bounds on a punt, it is brought back in bounds on the same yard line it went out on.

A coach may also direct the punter to kick the ball into the end zone so there will be little chance for a receiver to return it. If a punted ball goes into the end zone and then out of bounds, untouched by the receiving team, or if the player who receives the kick in his own end zone remains there, a touchback is called. Touchbacks do not involve a penalty or a score—they simply indicate that the ball is dead and the receivers will begin their offensive drive with a first and 10 on their own 20-yard line.

If the "pooch" or "coffin corner" punt succeeds, the ball
is spotted on the receiving team's 5-yard line or less, as
opposed to being on the 20-yard line after a touchback.
You can see, then, how advantageous it is for the kicking
team to get the ball as close as possible to the receiving
team's goal line.

You learned in Chapter 4 that the punter is used for
the kickoff following a safety. Normally the punter
stands about 15 yards *behind* the line of scrimmage to
punt. On a safety kick the punter is on the line along
with his teammates, like the placekicker on a kickoff.

The Return

The receiver has several options. He can make no
attempt to catch the ball if he thinks it's going out of
bounds at the sidelines. He can let the ball come to a stop
in bounds, without any member of his team trying to
gain possession of it. If the ball comes to a stop before
anyone touches it it will be whistled "dead." If a member
of the kicking team "downs" the ball by touching it
before a member of the receiving team does, the ball will
be ruled "dead" at that spot.

If the kick is in the end zone, the receiver can either
catch the ball and remain there or let it go and hope it
goes out of the end zone for a touchback.

Or he can extend one arm above his head and wave it
from side to side, signaling a **fair catch**. This means no
member of the kicking team may touch or tackle him,
for he must be allowed to catch the ball unmolested. His
part of the deal is he can't advance the ball; it is blown
dead as soon as he catches it. If he drops it, however, or
it touches a member of the receiving team, it is a loose
ball and may be recovered and advanced by any player
of either team.

A receiver's only other alternative is to attempt to
catch it and run. The average punt return is just short of
13 yards. It is hoped the ball carrier is tackled before he
gets back upfield to where the punter is, but in case he
isn't, the punter must try to bring him down.

The Placekicker (PK)

If a team needs a kickoff, field goal, point-after touch-down or a fair-catch kick, it calls on the placekicker.

From the 35-yard line, he kicks off to start the game or second half, either by placing the ball on a tee or having a teammate hold the ball on the ground.

The placekicker lines up about ten yards behind the ball, and his teammates line up on either side of him across the field. Before his foot makes contact with the ball, the other ten players must be behind the line of scrimmage (the forward-most point of the ball as it rests on the ground or tee before the kick), or the team will be assessed a five yard penalty for "offsides." This is a free kick, so the receiving team's line is ten yards ahead of the kicking team's, and there is a receiver (or two) called a "deep man," 50 or 60 yards away from the ball.

Photo courtesy of Tom Alberi/Detroit Lions.

After the referee blows his whistle and signals the play to begin, the placekicker kicks the ball in either a "head-on" or "sidewinder" style (like a soccer player). Either way, he may kick the ball with or without a shoe.

Kickoffs average 60 yards, so they go to about the defenders' 5-yard line. As soon as the placekicker kicks, his teammates run downfield to get to the receiver as soon as possible. Here again, the hang time is very important. The placekicker usually remains at about midfield, and is the kicking team's last hope of defense against the advancing ball carrier.

To prevent a good runback, the placekicker tries to kick the ball into the opposing team's end zone. If the ball goes out of bounds behind the goal line, a touchback will be signalled. If the receiver gains possession of the ball in the end zone, he can either run out with it or "down it"—by going down on one knee. If he thinks he can get beyond the 20-yard line—where the ball would be placed if he stayed in the end zone—he'll choose to run and hope to get more yardage and better field position for his team. A teammate often yells advice to the receiver, telling him whether to stay or run. The kicking team would normally rather have the ball dead on the receivers' 20-yard line than let them catch it and run it back upfield for a big gain, or worse yet, a touchdown.

A kickoff is also a touchback when the ball enters the opposing team's end zone and goes out of bounds before the kicking team can gain possession.

There is one more thing you should know about kickoffs. You've learned that when a punt goes out of bounds along the sidelines, the ball is brought back in bounds at the exact yard line as it went out. This can also apply to kickoffs, but not necessarily. When a kickoff goes out of bounds, the receiving team has the option of taking the ball at the same yard line it went out on, like a punt, or 30 yards from the spot of the kick. It will naturally choose the one closer to its opponent's goal line. This same procedure is used in kickoffs following point-after touchdown attempts and successful field goals, unless the coach requests an onside kick. Let me explain the onside kick.

On a kickoff the kicking team can get possession of

the ball if one of its members recovers it after it has
gone at least 10 yards downfield, or if it has been touched
by a member of the receiving team. Usually, the kicking
team wants to kick the ball deep into its opponent's territory, but sometimes it needs to get quick possession of
the ball—if the clock is ticking away, for instance, and
the team is losing. In this case, the team would try an
onside kick. This kind of kick is low and squiggly and is
intended to go the minimum ten yards, but not much
more, so the kicking team can get to the ball and recover
it. If the ball goes out of bounds, the kickers are penalized five yards and must kick it again from the 30-yard
line. If the re-kicked ball goes out of bounds, the receiving team has the same option as with a normal kickoff. If the kickoff team does recover the ball on an onside kick, it has good field position and a reasonable
chance to score during its turn on offense. If it fails, it
gives the receiving team even better field position.

The only time a kick off is not from the 35-yard line
(other than following a safety, when it is from the
20-yard line) is when a personal foul, unsportsmanlike
conduct, or obvious unfair act is committed during a
scoring play. The penalty for these infractions is assessed
on the following kickoff.

In addition to kickoffs, the placekicker is used for
field-goals and point-after touchdown (PAT) attempts.
On field-goal attempts the center snaps the ball to the
holder, usually a quarterback, who is down on one knee
seven yards behind the line of scrimmage. He quickly
props the ball on the ground so it can be kicked before
the defenders can rush in and knock it down. On field
goal and point-after touchdown attempts, the placekicker
is twice as close to the defensive line as the punter would
be during a punt, so he must get the ball kicked twice as
fast to prevent its being blocked by a defender.

On point-after touchdown attempts, the ball is placed
on the solid 2-yard line in the middle of the field. The
holder, usually the same one as for the field goal attempt,
receives the snap on the 10-yard line and quickly places it
in position on the ground for the placekicker.

To allow freedom of movement, the punter and placekicker have minimal padding. Because of this, they are
vulnerable both during and following a kick, so the

penalties are severe to defenders who violate the restrictions meant to protect them. (see Chapter 11—"Roughing the Kicker" and "Running into the Kicker").

One last reminder about field goal attempts and PATs. The ball is still live if it touches the goal post, unlike the punted ball, which is ruled dead.

The most important factor prior to any kick is getting the ball centered properly into the hands of the holder and/or punter. The timing and placement of the ball can mean the difference between success and failure.

The Fair Catch Kick

I purposely left the fair catch kick out of Chapter 3 because I didn't want to confuse you earlier, but I want to explain it here.

A field goal may be scored on a fair catch kick, which is a free kick, without a tee, on the play following a fair catch. It is done from the yard line of the catch, not from seven yards back of the line of scrimmage like a normal field goal attempt. It may be by placekick or drop kick, but the placekick is more logical because it has the lower trajectory and usually goes farther. Since it is a free kick, the defenders must line up at least 10 yards away from the ball. They are giving up the right to rush the kicker (like they can in a field goal attempt and point-after touchdown) while the kickers are giving up the ball after the kick (they would normally have a first and 10 following a fair catch). A fair catch kick could be used near the end of a half if the receiving team doesn't have enough time to move the ball downfield for a regular field goal attempt. It is seldom used, however, because most fair catches are made well out of field goal range, and the normal play in this situation is a Hail Mary (see Glossary).

9

Alignments and Formations

Coaches have a great deal of freedom to arrange their eleven players on the field. The offensive arrangement of players is called the **formation** or set. **Alignment** is the way the defensive players position themselves opposite the offense at the line of scrimmage before each scrimmage down starts. It's important to know this difference before we look at some actual alignments and formations.

Some players' places on the line of scrimmage never change (like most offensive guards). Others, like the tight ends, change more often, depending on the type of play that is planned. In the backfield, players are often shifted in and out, depending on the down. For example, one running back may be used on running plays and another on passing downs. Defenses respond accordingly, bringing in additional linemen or linebackers, to defend against the changing offensive formation.

The Neutral Zone

Let's look at the illustration of the offensive and defensive teams as they line up at the lines of scrimmage before the start of a play. Yes, you read me correctly. *Lines* of scrimmage. There are two because each team has one. We know the ball has to be placed on the field before the start of each down. A line of scrimmage is the imaginary line at *each* tip of the football as its rests on the ground, and it runs the width of the field from sideline to sideline. The line closer to a team as it lines up is that team's line of scrimmage.

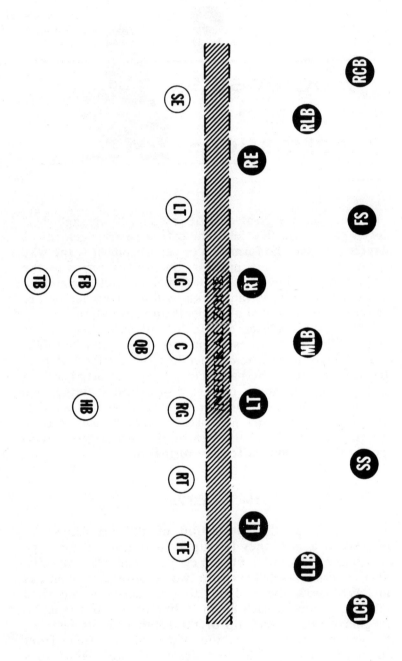

The neutral zone is the area the length of the football and extends from sideline to sideline. It is bounded by the two lines of scrimmage and the sidelines. If you think about it, if there was only one line of scrimmage the linemen's hands would touch and they would butt helmets. And where would the ball be placed? The center has to have his hand(s) ahead of his body to grasp the ball, so his hands are allowed in the neutral zone; all other players must be no closer than on *their own* line of scrimmage.

It's very important to understand this since every scrimmage play starts with a snap of the ball at the line of scrimmage. This is a most crucial time because it is then that many of the fouls are committed, like offside, false start, encroachment, illegal procedure and delay of game. Once the ball is in play the lines of scrimmage become one and it is the same as the defense used to line up on (the forward point of the football).

Calling the Shots

The offensive team's playbook contains dozens of plays and variations. Everything has a code. Sometimes a quarterback calls some of the plays, but usually they come from the bench. The quarterback coach or the head coach sends the plays either by signal or by a player sent into the game.

When a team takes possession of the ball and becomes the offense, the offensive platoon comes on the field. It forms a huddle before each down by gathering in a group far enough behind the line of scrimmage so that the defense can't hear the plans being made. (The exception to this is the "no-huddle offense" or "two- minute drill," when two or three plays are planned in a single huddle in order to save time).

The next play is either announced in the huddle, or the quarterback will say, "check with me." This means he will announce the next play in his signals after he looks over the defensive alignment. Each player knows what he is to do and where he is to be on that particular play. To keep the defensive team from knowing the exact moment when the ball will be snapped, a predetermined signal is given in the huddle so that only the offense knows when the center will hike the ball. This signal is usually the last word, phrase, or number in a short series called the "cadence" (also "signals" and "count").

The team lines up at the line of scrimmage in the formation (set) to be used on that play. If the quarterback sees the defense lining up as though it knows what the offensive play is going to be, he calls an "audible," also referred to as an "automatic" or a "check off." This means he makes a quick revision in the plans by calling a special number decided beforehand in the huddle, alerting his team to the change. The next call he makes gives the number of the new play, and finally, the last set of signals is for the ball to be centered. This last call may be the first, second or third number following the actual play number—anything to confuse the defense and cause them to go offside or be guilty of encroachment (see Chapter Eleven).

In summary, three numbers, words or phrases are decided in the huddle: the play to be used, when the ball is to be centered and the audible if necessary. Since the players already know the play announced in the huddle, the cadence only tells when the ball is to be snapped. No audible is used when the quarterback is satisfied with the way the defense is lining up.

Eligible Receivers

You've learned there must be a minimum of seven men on the offensive line of scrimmage before the ball is centered. There can be more, but only the two endmost men on the line and the three backs are eligible receivers. (The quarterback is an eligible receiver in the "shotgun" formation only). If there were eight on the line, the extra lineman would take away one of the backfield men; so instead of five eligible receivers (two linemen and three backs) there would only be four (two linemen and two backs). Therefore, seven is almost always the number used.

Interior Linemen

The interior linemen are the center, two tackles and two guards. No one except the center, who must put his hand(s) on the ball to center it, is allowed to move after lining up in a three- point stance. If there is any movement, the team will be penalized five yards for a false start.

Man in Motion

The other offensive players can move from one fixed position to another (called a "shift"). However, all except one—the man in motion, a back who moves in a parallel or retreating direction from the line of scrimmage—must come to a complete stop of movement (called "set position") for at least one second before the ball is snapped. Movement by two or more backs during the final second, or in a forward direction by the man in motion, results in a 5-yard penalty.

Photo courtesy of Tom Albert/Detroit Lions.

Defensive Play

Now to the defense. First of all, they are at a disadvantage because they don't usually know what the offensive play is going to be. Some plays, however, are easier to predict than others. For example, on a first and ten the offense could either run or pass. Films of an opponent's previous games might show that this team runs three out of four times on a first down, so it would be fairly predictable they would run in this case as well. On a third and ten, a team will pass more often than not. If the offense brings in a couple of wide receivers, however, the defense has to decide among several possibilities. They could put the pass rush on by bringing in linebackers who would rush the quarterback to sack him, or at least cause him to throw before he or his receivers are ready. Or they could bring in a couple of secondary players (cornerbacks or safeties) who would try to prevent a completed pass or a ten-yard run for a first down. Whatever they decide to do, however, the defensive players are always at a disadvantage because, whereas the offense knows what it's going to do, the defense must guess.

There can be any number of defensive players on the line of scrimmage. All eleven can be there, and sometimes they are. However, usually there are only three or four (see illustrations), and they are called down linemen. Before the start of a play, they go down in a three-point (one hand on the ground) or four-point (two hands) stance or in a semi-crouch with arms in an akimbo-like position. There are no restrictions on their alignment or motion before the snap, just as long as they are not guilty of "encroachment."

The defense has specific alignments it uses against certain offensive formations, but it can shift positions and move around at will. The defensive coordinator watches the offensive players as they go on the field for a play. If they're wide receivers, there might be a pass. If they're backs, a running play is more likely. The defensive coordinator signals to the defensive captain which alignment to use, but it is subject to change when the offensive team lines up. The captain of the defense is usually the middle linebacker because he has the best view of the offensive formation. He can make a change in the signaled alignment to better defend against an audible. As you recall, an audible is a quick change of plans by the quarterback at the line of scrimmage.

You're probably wondering why more plays don't work if the offense always knows exactly what it's going to do and the defense is only anticipating. The word is "execution." Even if every offensive player knows what he's to do on each play, there are extenuating circumstances that prevent a play from succeeding. There might be the unexpected double coverage on the planned receiver, or a sudden rush from the defense that makes the quarterback get rid of the ball quicker than he had planned. Let's say there's to be a pass from the quarterback on the 40-yard line to a receiver on the 15-yard line, five yards in from the sideline. Yes, they are that exact. After the snap, the receiver has to have time to get downfield and in position to catch the ball. If the quarterback's pass is hurried, it will probably be short of the target and either become incomplete or intercepted by a defensive player. Or, if the quarterback gets a good pass off, the receiver could slip, be double covered, have the ball batted away, or drop the ball. It's a matter of perfect timing for both the offense and defense.

Formations

Let's look at some illustrations of alternative formations. In Chapters 6, 7 and 8, you learned the letters for each player. For instance, "QB" is the abbreviation for quarterback, "SE" for split end, and so on. It might help to write in the names of each player as you study the offensive formations and defensive alignments.

In all the formations, the interior linemen maintain their same positions. Even though the split and the tight ends do not vary in the illustrations, they can be reversed in any of the sets. The flanker and the tight end are usually on the same side, but the flanker can line up on the weak side. The biggest variance is in the backs and their position relative to the quarterback.

Take a look at the formations, and you'll see the logic in their names. The "I" has the quarterback and two backs, the fullback and the tailback, lined up in an "I." The "single back" has only one backfield man. The "T" has the quarterback and three backs in an inverted "T," and the "wishbone" really looks like a chicken bone.

A person doesn't normally watch a game and say, "Oh! they're using the 'I' formation!" But it's interesting to know what an announcer is talking about when he says the offense is lining up in the "wishbone" or "pro" set.

Shotgun Formation

One offensive formation you will recognize every time is the **shotgun**. It's the only one in which the quarterback stands about five yards behind the center, instead of immediately in back of him. This formation gets its name because the the ball has to be snapped (shot back like a shell out of a gun) the five yards instead of handed back to the quarterback as in all other sets. It's the only formation where the quarterback is an eligible receiver. To be eligible to catch passes, a receiving player must be *at least* **one** yard behind the line of scrimmage when the ball is snapped. In all other formations except kicking plays, the quarterback is less than a yard behind the line.

The shotgun is used most often on passing plays, but is also freqently used by a team whose quarterback is being sacked repeatedly. The five yards between him and the line of scrimmage gives him a few more seconds to release the ball.

The Pro or Open Formation

The pro or open formation is the most common set in professional football. In the "pro" set, the flanker can run in one of the directions shown in this diagram. He has to be at least one yard behind the line of scrimmage and running in a parallel or retreating direction.

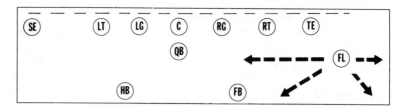

The I Formation

The "I" formation illustration shows what a shift—a movement by two or more players at one time—looks like. Remember, only one of them can be moving as the ball is centered, so two of the runners must stop all movement for one second prior to the snap. If they don't, the team is penalized five yards for illegal motion. You can see the tailback cannot be the man in motion because he's moving toward the line instead of parallel or away from it, so he will be one of the two who stops before the snap.

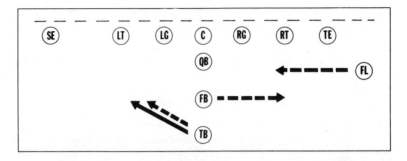

Other Offensive Sets

Below are the wing, T, wishbone, power I and single back.

Wing Formation

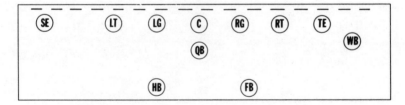

T Formation

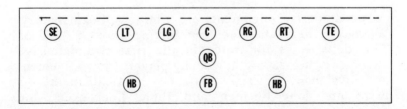

Wishbone Formation

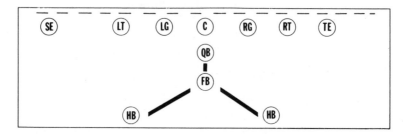

Power I Formation

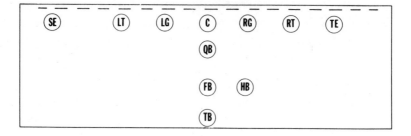

Single Back Formation

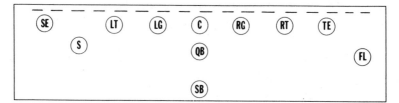

Defensive Alignments

The defensive alignments are almost self-explanatory. When you hear an announcer talking about a "4-3" or "3-4" defense, as illustrated in the first two defensive alignments, he's saying how many players (down linemen) and how many linebackers are on the field. In the 4-3 there are four linemen and three linebackers; the remaining four are backfield men. In the 3-4 there are three players on the line, four linebackers and four defensive backs.

3-4 Alignment

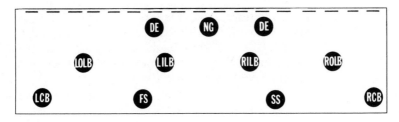

4-3 Alignment

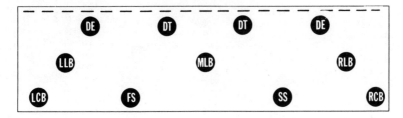

The Bears' Defense: The 4-6 Alignment

When Buddy Ryan was the defensive coordinator for the Chicago Bears, he originated the 4-6. You know from the previous two examples that this means there are four men on the line, six in the middle and one back.

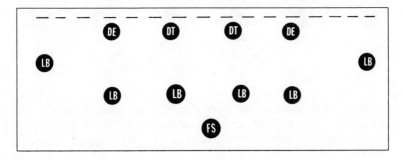

The Nickel and Dime Defenses

In the "nickel" defense, one player is taken either from the line or middle and an extra player is put in the secondary. In the "dime," two players are removed from the front two lines while two more players are placed in the backfield. Thus, one extra back, a "nickel," and two extra backs, a "dime." The more men in the secondary, the more a team expects a passing play.

The Nickel Defense

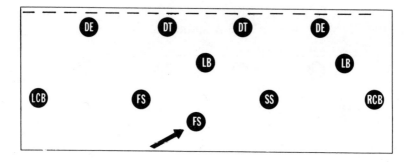

The Dime Defense

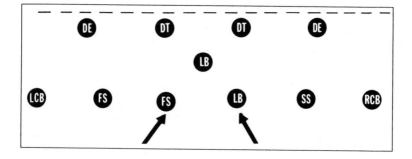

Now that you know why the offense and defense line up at the line of scrimmage the way they do, you'll enjoy watching the plays unfold and seeing who outmaneuvers whom.

10

The Officials

Every game has rules in order to make it fun and fair for all involved. Who's responsible for enforcing these rules in a football game? The zebra-striped men on the field. These law enforcers are hired and trained by the National Football League.

Applicants must have ten years of experience in football officiating, with five of them in major college games, before they can apply to the NFL. Chances are, many spent Saturday mornings officiating little league games and then moved on to high school junior varsity and varsity games before arriving at the college level. There is work behind the building of an officiating career.

Besides knowing all the rules, officials must be able to withstand mental and judgmental strains and the verbal abuse from players, coaches and fans. They also have to be in excellent physical condition. An average game has 130 plays, and the officials are in on every one, moving up and down the field constantly. In contrast, the "platoon" system keeps players on the field only about half the time.

The NFL puts the 117 officials into 16 squads of seven each (plus two pivot men who fill in wherever needed) and assigns a replay official to each squad. He is a permanent member and travels with the crew. The squads are responsible to the supervisor of officials and his four assistants.

Each official works one game a week with two weeks off during the season. For the 16-game season they earn from $600 to $2,000 per game, depending on seniority within the league.

You're probably wondering what they do the rest of the week. They have regular jobs just like everyone else. They're teachers, professors, high school principals, doctors, lawyers, insurance salesmen, and real estate brokers. Also, there is an oil company president, a bank president, a general contractor, a longshoreman, a patrolman, a pharmacist and a hospital administrator. Most have not been NFL players, but the few who were, played only a year or two.

What is the uniform of the day? Black and white striped shirt and socks, black belt and shoes, white knicker pants, and a baseball-like cap. The referee's cap is white while the others wear black. Each official is responsible for his own cleaning and mending. The NFL furnishes the entire uniform the first time and then replaces only the basics (shirt, pants, and cap) thereafter.

What equipment does an official need on the field? Besides a whistle, he has a yellow handkerchief, a marker, a card and a pencil. He blows the whistle only to stop or start a down. He throws the handkerchief on the field at the spot of a foul, and he throws the marker to indicate ball placement, like the spot of a fumble (see Glossary). He carries the card and pencil in a pocket to record each foul he calls and the subsequent penalty. In addition, the umpire has a paging device for communicating with the replay official.

The officials receive their assignment two weeks in advance, and must go a day early to review film of the crew's previous game. When they travel from their homes to games and back home again, the NFL makes the hotel reservations and books their flights. For a Sunday game they arrive in their assigned city on Saturday and are at the stadium about two hours before game time. The entire crew is required to appear on the field 30 minutes before the opening kickoff.

Each official specializes and works the same position every game. For instance, one who is listed as a back judge will only officiate as a back judge unless an injury or illness dictates a reshuffling. Each squad has a "disaster" plan if one or more of its members is injured or ill. This can happen by being knocked down by a runner, getting in the way of a tackle, or catching the flu on game day.

How does the NFL know if each official is doing his job? The supervisor of officials staff spends several hours each week during the season looking at the films of every game. Each official is graded, and the top ones are selected for the playoffs, where they receive $5,000 per game and $7,500 for the Super Bowl. Although they are expected to make perfect calls on every play, they are human and do make some mistakes. In fact, some teams have blamed losses on poor officiating.

After debating the idea of instant replay cameras to check certain calls by the officials, the team owners voted in 1986 to add an extra official, called the replay official, for this purpose. He is a former NFL or college official who can overrule the calls of the other officials, but does so only when the replay shows unquestionable visible proof involving possession, most plays governed by the sidelines, goal lines, end lines and line of scrimmage (for example, whether the ball carrier is in or out of bounds, or whether a player has scored a touchdown) and easily detectable infractions on replays (for example, more than 11 men on one team).

You're probably wondering why *all* the fouls aren't called from the private booth above the field where the replay official sits. That's a logical thought, but coaches and players agree that the officials on the field are in a better position to see most of the rule infractions.

Positions of the Officials

How can you distinguish one official from the other when watching a game? Before the start of each play you can see where the officials position themselves on the field. But easier yet, there are white numbers and letters on the front and back of each official's shirt. The numbers identify the name of the official on the NFL roster, and the letters show his job. For example, if an official comes out on the field with U 101 on his shirt, you'll know immediately that he's an umpire. By looking up number 101 under "OFFICIALS" in *Gameday*, the stadium program, you'll see that his name is Bob Boylston. There is no set system of numbering, so an official may request a different number at the beginning of each season.

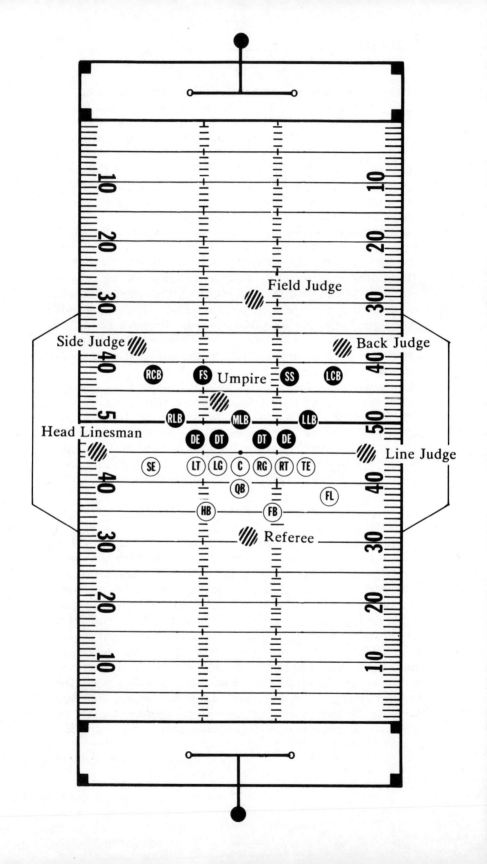

The officials are positioned around the area of play in order to make sure rule infractions don't go unnoticed. As you look at the field, you will see only one official, the referee, on the side of the offense. There are two on the line of scrimmage, the line judge on one side of the field and the head linesman on the other. The other four officials are on the defensive side of the line. Each one has certain responsibilities and a specific place to be when a play begins.

The Referee

The referee is the man in charge and is captain of the squad. He wears a white cap and a wireless microphone and stands 10 to 15 yards behind the quarterback and off to the side. If the quarterback is right-handed, the referee probably will be on his right side. He is responsible for:

- focussing on the quarterback;
- giving signals and announcing all fouls and having final authority for rule interpretations;
- explaining a team's options on a penalty, unless the penalty is automatic;
- keeping track of the number of downs;
- calling "roughing the passer" or "roughing the kicker" penalties;
- ruling on whether a loose ball is the result of a quarterback fumble or an incompleted pass;
- notifying coaches when their teams have used up their time-outs and letting both coaches know when two-minutes remain in a half;
- signaling when to stop and start the game clock and second clock;
- starting and stopping the game.

Three minutes prior to the start of a game, the referee calls the team captains onto the field. The official flips a coin, and the visiting team calls either heads or tails. The winner of the call gets to choose whether his team will receive the kickoff or defend a particular goal, and the loser has the same choice the second half. The team that receives the kickoff the first half of the game will most likely kick off to the other team to start the second half, but the captains of both teams must inform the referee of their respective choices immediately prior to the start of the second half. He then comes on the field and indicates who will be the receiving team.

The Umpire

The umpire stands about five yards behind the middle defensive lineman. He is responsible for:

- checking the legality of equipment.
- watching contact actions of players on the line of scrimmage.
- looking for false starts by offensive linemen.
- noting whether linemen are illegally downfield on passes.
- ruling on trapped or incompleted passes.
- wearing a paging device and acting as liaison between the replay official and referee.

The Head Linesman

The head linesman stands on the line of scrimmage. He is responsible for:

- ruling on "offside" and "encroachment."
- ruling on sideline plays on his side of the field.
- watching the closest running back.
- helping the referee keep track of the number of downs.
- marking the forward point of the ball with his foot.
- supervising the chain crew.
- watching the actions of the blockers and defenders on his side of the field.

The Line Judge

The line judge straddles the line of scrimmage opposite the head linesman. He is responsible for:

- ruling on "offside" and "encroachment."
- watching the actions of the blockers and defenders on his side of the field.
- watching the closest running back.
- acting as backup timekeeper to the clock operator.
- observing pass receivers until they move at least seven yards downfield.
- ruling on whether a passer is behind or beyond the line of scrimmage when a pass is made.
- watching the kicking team as they move downfield to cover the kick.
- focusing on punts to make sure only the two end men move downfield before the ball is kicked.
- ruling on sideline plays on his side of the field.

The Side Judge

The side judge stands 17 yards deep on the same side of the field as the head linesman. He is responsible for:

- watching the wide receiver on his side.
- making in-bounds and out-of-bounds calls on catches and runing plays near his sideline.
- checking for "clipping" on punt returns.
- ruling on "pass interference."
- making decisions involving a loose ball beyond the line of scrimmage.
- ruling on plays involving pass receivers and runners.

The Back Judge

The back judge stands 17 yards deep on the same side of the field as the line judge. He has the same responsibilities as the side judge and he helps the field judge rule on field goals and extra point kicks.

The Field Judge

The field judge stands mid-way on the field, 25 yards deep on the defensive side. He is responsible for:

- focusing on the tight end, his blocks, and the actions taken to knock him off course.
- timing the interval between plays on the second clock as well as the interval between quarters, when the teams are changing goal lines to defend.
- ruling on field goals and extra point kicks.
- calling "pass interference," "fair catch" infractions and "clipping" on kick returns.

The Replay Official

The replay official sits in a private booth in the press box and views the game on two monitors. If he doesn't question a call, play on the field continues. If he believes an error may have been made, he contacts the umpire by a paging device and play is stopped while he reviews the play in question. There is also an NFL staff member and a technician he can confer with. Whatever his decision, he notifies the umpire, and the umpire informs the referee who makes the public announcement. The replay official's decision is final. His authority includes those plays involving possession, such as interceptions, receptions, fumbles, muffs, the line of scrimmage, goal lines and the end lines and sidelines, like out-of-bounds. The rest of the fouls called by field officials are not reviewed for possible reversal.

The Assistant Officials (Chain Crew)

The seven assistant officials are positioned along the sidelines. They are hired by the home team and approved by the NFL. Two are responsible for the down indicators (see Glossary), two for the yardage chain (see Glossary—"chain crew"), one for the X pole (drive start) that shows where a team's ball possession originates, one for the forward stake indicator and the last one for recording all fouls and penalties. Their uniform is different from the other officials in that they wear a white shirt with a checked or striped vest.

The Ball Boys

The ball boys are the uniformly dressed attendants who are responsible for the game balls on the sidelines. Their duty is to have a new and/or clean ball ready for play at all times.

Now that you've seen what the officials' main responsibilities are, their jobs don't look so easy, do they? Maybe we'll think twice next time we feel like booing their decisions. Disagreeing with the officials is one thing, but booing is something entirely different. Each official can't be everywhere he's supposed to be all the time, but he *is* on the field near the action while we're sitting in the stands or watching on television.

NFL Official's Game Card

There's more to officiating than looking for fouls and assessing penalties. Officials have to write out reports which include a list of every penalty that was called during the game. A copy of an actual official's game card is reproduced on the next page.

NFL OFFICIAL'S GAME CARD

HOME TEAM _____

JERSEY COLOR (   )

DATE _____ GAME NO _____

CAPT _____

CAPT _____

_____

TOSS _____

	FIRST HALF		**TIME OUT**		SECOND HALF	
1	2	3	1	2		3

HOME TEAM

QT.	TIME REMAIN	FOUL	OFF. DEF.	PLYR NO	ACC DEC.	# CLD

11

Penalties and Signals

Just as there are rules in every kind of game, there must also be punishments for violations. You already know who the law enforcers are, but what about the infractions? What are they and how are they penalized?

A foul is any violation of a playing rule. The purpose of a penalty for a foul is to move the guilty team farther away from the offended team's goal line.

There are over 70 penalties that may be assessed. You learned in the previous chapter all about the officials. You know the name of each, his basic position on the field, and his main responsibilities. When an official sees a violation, he throws his penalty flag on the ground at the spot of the foul. After the whistle is blown at the end of the play, the official who saw the infraction reports it to the referee who:

- informs the team captains;
- tells the wronged team its options and the yardage that would be gained or lost by accepting or declining the penalty;
- signals and announces to the press box what the foul is, the number of the guilty player if known, the yards penalized for it and the down. If the penalty is accepted by the offended team, the penalty yardage is assessed and the same down is usually played over. If it is refused, the referee announces this and the next down is played as though no penalty occurred.

Refusing a Penalty

You're probably wondering why a team would ever refuse a foul against its opponent. Let me give you an example. Suppose the offense has a first down and 10 yards to go. On the next play from scrimmage, the offense gains nine yards, but the defense was guilty of being offside, a five-yard penalty. If the penalty is accepted, the ball is taken back to the line of scrimmage of the play just completed and moved five yards toward the defenders' goal line. Now it is first down with five yards to go for a first down (instead of 10), because the offense has gained five yards from its opponents' penalty. Also, if the penalty is accepted, the same down is replayed.

If the offense declines the penalty, the ball is left where it was when the play was blown dead— nine yards beyond the line of scrimmage—and the down is not replayed. So the next down, the second in this case, is played as though no penalty occurred. It is now second down and one yard to go for a first down, instead of first down and five, and the ball is four yards closer to the opponents' goal line. In other words, the ball is nine yards from the previous play's line of scrimmage, instead of the five it would be if the penalty were accepted.

As a rule of thumb, if a team gains more yardage on a play than what a penalty would give, it refuses it because the name of the game is to cross the opponents' goal line in any way possible, and every yard counts. An exception to this rule occurs when the offense breaks a rule during a third down. When the offense fails to make a first down, the defense usually declines the penalty, whatever it is, so that third down is not played over again. This forces the offense into a fourth down punting situation.

There are no options with two fouls which occur before the ball is put into play—**false start**, an offensive foul, and **encroachment**, a defensive foul. The penalty for both of these fouls is five yards. The required yardage is walked off, the ball placed, and the down played over.

Measuring the Assessment

The spot of enforcement is the starting place at which penalty yardage is measured. Depending upon the foul, the penalty yardage is measured from one of four basic spots on the field:

• **Exact.** The exact spot where the foul was committed.

Example: "Defensive pass interference."

• **Previous.** The spot where the ball was last put in play.

Example: "Offensive pass interference."

• **Loose Ball.** The spot where the act of a temporarily loose ball connected with the foul occurred.

Example: During a fumble, kick, pass or process of centering the ball—whenever the ball is briefly not in a player's possession.

• **Succeeding.** The spot where the ball would next be in play if no penalty were enforced.

Example: "Unsportsmanlike conduct" when the ball is dead. In other words, fouls occurring between downs.

Don't be alarmed. You don't have to memorize this, but as you watch more games you'll become aware that all penalties aren't marked off from the same place. Each penalty dictates its own spot of enforcement.

Near the Goal Line

I would like to mention one other point about penalties. If a penalty would move the ball more than half the distance to the fouling team's goal line, the ball is placed midway between the goal line and the spot of enforcement. For example, suppose the line of scrimmage is the defensive 10-yard line, and on the next play a defender roughs the quarterback after a pass. The penalty is 15 yards, but that would push the defense back into the end zone. So the rule states that the ball can be put only halfway to the goal line, or on the 5-yard line, since that's halfway from the original line of scrimmage on the 10.

Let's go one step further. If the defense commits the same foul on the next play, the ball would be placed on the 2-1/2-yard line, halfway between the 5-yard line and the goal line. It may sound as if the offenders are unfairly getting a break on the penalty yardage, but there's a purpose to this rule: a touchdown cannot be scored as the result of a penalty. An exception to this rule is a foul intended to prevent a score through an unfair act, such as an opposing player on the sidelines stepping onto the field and tripping the ball carrier who is going for a sure touchdown.

Types of Fouls

The *Official NFL Rules Book* lists all the fouls and the yards penalized for each. There are four types of fouls:

- **Continuing action.** Occurring immediately after a down ends, like an offensive clip after the ball carrier has run out of bounds;
- **Multiple.** Two or more fouls by the same team during the same down;
- **Double.** A foul by each team during the same down;
- **Foul Between Downs.** A foul after a down has definitely ended but before the next begins, like an offensive foul after a touchdown has been scored.

Most fouls are self-explanatory, like "delay of game," "defensive holding," "offside" or "roughing the kicker." I've listed the most common ones you'll see in a game, and the referee's hand signals are shown next to each description. Study them, and in no time at all you'll know what the infraction is by the referee's signal before it's even announced.

PERSONAL FOUL
One wrist striking the other above head
followed by hand striking back of calf.

Clipping

Clipping is throwing oneself across the back of an opponent's leg, or charging or falling into the back of an opponent below the waist, after approaching from behind; the opponent is not a runner, or the play is not a close line play. The offense is a personal foul unless done in close line play where it is permitted three yards on either side of the line of scrimmage, between the line where the offensive tackles line up (provided the offensive lineman clips a defender who is lined up no more than one position away.)

Penalty—15 yards from the point where the clip occurs.

Delay of Game

The offensive team has 45 seconds (25 seconds following timeouts, injuries or other unusual delays) to begin the next down. If it takes any longer to put the ball in play, a "delay of game" is called.

Penalty—5 yards.

Grasping an Opponent's Face Mask

Even if a tackler accidentally does it, it is not allowed. The referee signals for a personal foul and then makes a pulling motion with a fist, as if pulling a face mask.

Penalty—5 yards if incidental and not an automatic first down; 15 yards if deliberate and an automatic first down if the penalty is against the defensive team.

Encroachment

Before the ball is centered, a defensive player may enter the neutral zone and retreat without a penalty, but he is guilty of "encroachment" if he draws an opponent offside or makes contact with an opponent.

Penalty—5 yards.

OFFSIDE or ENCROACHING

Offside

A player from either team is "offside" if any part of his body is beyond the team's line of scrimmage when the ball is centered.

Penalty—5 yards.

Holding—Defensive

A defensive player cannot hold an opponent other than the ball carrier or a player pretending to be the ball carrier.

Penalty—5 yards and an automatic first down.

Holding—Offensive

The ball carrier is the only offensive player who may use his hands to ward off opponents. No other offensive player may encircle or obstruct an opponent with his arms or hands. Signal is same for offensive and defensive holding.

Penalty—10 yards.

Illegal Block in the Back Above the Waist

It is illegal to block or push in the back above the waist. This foul is usually called on punts or kickoffs.

Penalty—10 yards from the point where the illegal block occurs.

Illegal Crackback Block

A wide receiver cannot clip a defender anywhere on the field, or block a defender below the waist within five yards of either side of the line of scrimmage when the defender is moving toward the ball.

Penalty—15 yards.

ILLEGAL CRACKBACK

Illegal Motion

Only one offensive player (who must be a back) may move during the final second before the ball is centered. He must be moving in a parallel direction to, or retreating from, the line of scrimmage and must be no closer than one yard to it. A back who moves during this final second is called the "man in motion," and he is guilty of "illegal motion" if he moves in a forward direction or if more than one back is moving.

ILLEGAL MOTION AT SNAP

Penalty—5 yards.

False Start

An offensive lineman may not break his three-point stance, nor may any offensive player simulate the start of a down, before the ball is centered.

Penalty—5 yards.

FALSE START, ILLEGAL SHIFT, ILLEGAL PROCEDURE, ILLEGAL FORMATION, or KICKOFF OR SAFETY KICK OUT OF BOUNDS

Ineligible Receiver Downfield

The offensive team whose players are eligible to catch a pass are the two endmost linemen and the players in the backfield who are at least one yard in back of the line of scrimmage. All others are "ineligible receivers" who may not advance more than one yard beyond the line of scrimmage before the ball leaves the passer's hands. However, they become eligible if the ball is touched by any eligible receiver.

Penalty—10 yards.

Intentional Grounding

A quarterback or other passer cannot throw the ball into the ground solely to keep from losing yardage under threat from a defensive player.

Penalty—10 yards and loss of down, but if the foul occurs more than ten yards behind the line of scrimmage, the penalty is a loss of down at the spot of the foul. If intentional grounding is committed in the end zone, the result is a safety.

Pass Interference

Players on both teams have an equal right to catch a passed ball. Neither the intended receiver nor the defender, however, is allowed to hold or shove his opponent, or block his path as he goes for the ball.

Penalty—Offensive: 10 yards from the previous spot. Defensive: automatic first down at the spot of the foul. If the defensive interference is committed in the end zone, the ball is placed on the one-yard line.

Piling On

A defender is not allowed to fall on a runner (or any downed opponent) when the ball is dead.

Penalty—15 yards and an automatic first down.

Roughing the Kicker

Intentionally running into the kicker is not permitted.

Penalty—15 yards and an automatic first down for the kicking team.

Roughing the Passer

After a passer releases the ball, a defensive player may not run into him if the defender has a reasonable chance to stop his momentum in his attempt to block the pass or tackle the passer.

Penalty—15 yards and an automatic first down. A player may be disqualified if the violation is considered flagrant.

Running into the Kicker

A defender is not permitted to run into a punter or field goal kicker without first blocking or touching the ball, unless contact was caused by the kicker himself or by the block of one of his teammates.

Penalty—5 yards and no automatic first down for the kicking team.

Unnecessary Roughness

Intentionally violent acts, such as tackling a runner out of bounds, tackling a player obviously uninvolved in the play, butting with the helmet, piling on, striking with the fists, kicking or kneeing, are considered personal fouls. The referee gives the personal foul signal and then gives a second signal to identify the exact infraction.

Penalty—15 yards and an automatic first down if the penalty is called against the defensive team; disqualification for a player who "flagrantly" butts, spears or rams an opponent.

Unsportsmanlike Conduct

Any conduct the officials consider to be contrary to the principles of sportsmanship, such as abusive language or gestures from a player or a member of the coaching staff, a kicker or holder simulating roughness or excessive celebration by individual players or groups of players.

Penalty—15 yards and an automatic first down if the penalty is called against the defensive team; disqualification when the violation is considered flagrant.

**UNSPORTSMANLIKE
CONDUCT**

12

Equipment

Are you irritated when one of your players tries to intercept a pass and fails? Are you ready to scream after he lets a loose ball get away? Don't. Take a good look at him and all his equipment, especially his arms and hands, and you'll understand why it's not easy to hold onto the ball. Even if a player had no encumbrances, the irregular shape of the ball makes its bounces unpredictable and difficult to catch and hold onto.

Before a player can step on the field, he has to dress. This covering adds 15 to 20 pounds to his weight.

What are the pieces of equipment a player puts on before he's ready to play?

1. First, he has his feet, ankles, arms and/or chest wrapped with a special polyester adhesive tape. Most players are bandaged, and the amount and areas are usually determined by the trainer.

2. Jockstrap.

3. Underwear-like girdle with hip pads.

4. Pants with pockets for knee and thigh pads.

5. Stockings.

6. Shoes. They are required even though shoeless kicking is permitted. The style varies according to the playing surface and personal preference. On artificial grass (a type of indoor-outdoor carpeting), the players usually wear a 150-stud turf shoe that has a bottom like a rubber spiked golf shoe. On a natural grass field, shoes with three metal cleats are worn.

Illustration of equipment a typical player wears.

Photo of Bubba Paris being taped.

7. Flac jacket (rib and kidney protector).
8. Shoulder pads.
9. Arm, elbow and hand pads.
10. Jersey.
11. Neck roll (optional).
12. Helmet with face mask, chin strap and an optional mouth guard.

For outdoor games in cold weather, many receivers wear black scuba-style gloves and linemen often wear golf gloves under their protective hand padding. Before cold weather games many players coat their skin with a cream designed to prevent frostbite and windburn.

Now you know the equipment a player needs for a football game and the order in which he puts each piece on. What do you think it costs a franchise to put a player on the field? After itemizing each piece of equipment of a Detroit Lions player, I came up with about $725, for a full rookie uniform. Every piece, however, doesn't have to be replaced each year. For instance, a helmet could last half a season, four seasons, or a lifetime, depending on the position of the player and wear. If a player has been injured and needs a special injury pad, that's another $375. Also, this doesn't count all the tape used on each player. So you can see these guys don't come cheaply dressed.

Uniforms

Teams furnish each player two sets of uniforms, called "home" and "away." One is usually white and the other, the team colors. The home team has the choice of color and notifies the opposing teams beforehand of its selection so the visitors will wear contrasting colors.

There are two jerseys with each uniform. Players used to wear the tearaway kind so they could keep running after their shirts were literally ripped off their backs, but that type has been banned. Still, because of possible rips during a game, some linemen and running backs not only have a third jersey, but also have them tailored for a tighter fit so there is no slack for grabbing by an opponent.

Jerseys cannot be too similar in color to the ball. Imagine how confusing it would be for everyone if the football blended in with a uniform. Every team in the league would want the same color as the ball for camouflage purposes.

Names and Numbers

Besides jersey colors, there are also requirements for the numerals and names. They must be in a contrasting color to the jerseys for easy identification of each player. The numbers must be eight inches long and four inches wide. In addition, most teams have numbers on the shoulders or upper arms for easy recognition by the broadcasters who are above the field. A player's last name appears on the back of the jersey above the numerals.

There is also a system for numbering the players that makes it easy for the officials and fans to identify them. Numbers are assigned to players according to the position they play and are as follows:

1-19—quarterbacks and kickers
20-49—running backs and defensive backs
50-59—centers and linebackers
60-79—interior linemen (including centers) and defensive linemen
80-89—wide receivers and tight ends
90-99—defensive linemen and linebackers

No two players on the same team may have identical numbers, but some players play two positions. Whenever a player comes into the game to play a position with a number that would make him ineligible (for example, tackle to end), he must report the change to the referee or his team will be assessed a five yard penalty for "failure to report change of eligibility," and he will be required to go out of the game for one play.

When you're watching a game and see two offensive players whose numbers are in the 80's coming in for a play, you know they're either wide receivers or tight ends. As wide receivers, they could be split ends (who line up on the line) or flankers (who line up behind the line and usually on the same side of the ball as the tight end). This means there will probably be a pass play because that's their specialty. Therefore, the defense lines up accordingly. If the two players are numbered 33 and 82, a running back and a wide receiver or tight end, the defense has to try and decide whether the offense is going to run or pass. The down, the yardage and the field position will generally determine the type of play called.

Equipment Manager

A team's equipment manager is one of the most important people on the staff because he is responsible for all the gear. He and his assistants are in charge of making sure every piece of equipment is in playing condition.

Dan Jaroshewich, equipment manager for the Detroit Lions, told me what his job entailed for "away" games. The day before departure, he posts a list on the bulletin board of the things each player is to pack—helmet, pads, shoes, etc.—in his own team duffle bag. While collecting the bags beside the lockers, his assistant checks each one. All remaining pieces of equipment are packed separately. The equipment weighs about 5,000 pounds if the team is going to a game in a mild climate or indoor facility, or about 7,500 pounds if it's going to a cold outdoor area where parkas, gloves and thermals are needed. Upon arrival at the team's destination, both he and his assistant go directly to the stadium with the equipment, unpack it, and put each player's gear into his own personal locker. After the game, he must see that everything is bagged up and nothing forgotten.

I don't envy his job, because he has every rip and lost piece of equipment for 45 young men to deal with. (There are twice that many in training camp). I couldn't keep up with the mending for three kids—much less 45—and I was a Home Ec major. I'm afraid if the players were my responsibility, they'd appear on the field wearing safety pins. True, he doesn't sit down like Grandma Moses and hand-sew every tear, but it's his responsibility to check all the equipment and send out the necessary pieces to be repaired.

And one more thing. How would you like to buy laundry detergent, bleach and fabric softener in five-gallon containers, or lift 85 pounds of wet clothes out of a washing machine and into a dryer not once, but *five times* after every game and practice? I know I would protest, but then again I expect time-and-a-half for doing two or three piddling washings a week.

Besides doing all the immediate work in preparation for the games, both home and away, the equipment manager attends sporting goods shows looking for the newest and safest pieces available, always aware of the close correlation between sound equipment and the number and intensity of injuries. Although he does the procuring, the players have options on many of the pieces.

For example, the style of face mask is a personal preference. It can be an open cage (no vertical bar above the nose) with two or three horizontal bars, or a closed cage with a nose bridge (vertical bar running the length of the mask over the nose) with two, three or four horizontal bars. Usually the quarterbacks, running backs, wide receivers and defensive backfield men choose the open cage type because of better visibility. Linemen, because of closer contact, usually prefer the closed cage type to keep fingers and hands out of their eyes.

A quarterback's shoulder pads are smaller and lighter than those of the other players, so his arm will have freer movement; thus, he chooses the style he's most comfortable in. Hip pads are required, but shin guards are optional. Some linemen wear padded gloves; others, unpadded. Many prefer having their hands taped. A player's past and present injuries play a significant part in his equipment options, as well as the amount of taping necessary.

Players' Safety

What's the difference whether a player hits with his helmet or shoulder pads? It's been proven that a player with a good pair of pads can hit harder through his shoulder and/or chest than through his head, with much less risk of serious, irreversible injury to himself or to his opponent.

According to Mike Black, a former punter for Arizona State University and the Detroit Lions, "Football is one of the most safety-conscious sports around. The two most important pieces of equipment to come forth in modern football are the flac jacket and the Anderson knee brace, but the helmet is still the most important." Helmets must be of the best construction to minimize the chance of severe neck and brain injuries. Usually the shell is made out of a tough plastic called polycarbonate alloy and must be approved by the National Operating Committee on Standards for Athletic Equipment (NOCSAE).

NOCSAE was formed in 1969 to reduce injuries by establishing equipment standards through scientific research. Wayne State University in Detroit, long a leader in head injury and protection mechanics, was chosen to direct the research. Dr. Voigt Hodgson, a faculty member of the Department of Neurosurgery, has done studies in the area of head and neck injury for 30 years and has been a principal investigator for NOCSAE almost since its inception. He said that since head injuries are the source of greatest concern in football, the helmet has been the primary target for research. There has been a 65 per cent decrease in fatal head injuries among high school players since the inception of NOCSAE, and a reduction of permanent damage to the cervical cord from 34 players in 1976 to 3 in 1986.

The testing equipment is very sophisticated and has greatly reduced the number of fatal head injuries in all levels of play. Hodgson said the helmet could be made even safer by enlarging it with more padding, but then it would become too heavy and would increase the risk of neck injury. "We make what is playable as safe as possible," he said.

NOCSAE also endorses a new mask that was designed and patented by John Butash of Royal Oak, Michigan. It is the first significant change to football face masks in more than 30 years, and is being worn by players in all levels of play, from Little League to the NFL. It has scores of free-spinning, shatterproof plastic beads that overlay the face mask. Because the beads spin, it's virtually impossible to grab the mask from any angle. Also, when the mask hits the turf or an opposing player, the spinning of the beads reduces the possibility of injury caused by impact situations. It will not only lower facial injuries, but also keep the hazards of neck injuries to a minimum.

The Official Football

The NFL has contracted with Wilson Sporting Goods since 1941 to make all the footballs for the league. A team purchases about 500 a year. Speaking of footballs, do you know why the net is raised behind the uprights whenever a field goal or point-after touchdown is attempted? It isn't because of the cost of the balls, but rather to save on the number of security guards needed to stop the fans from fighting over a ball kicked into the stands.

The home team must have 24 footballs ready to be checked by the referee two hours before game time. They must be Wilson balls with the NFL name stamped on them, and they must bear the signature of the commissioner of the league. Twelve are put into play during each half, and then all are used later for practice.

We know what a football looks like—oblong and pointed at both ends—but what is its exact size and what is it made of? It is 11 to 11-1/4 inches long (leather stretches) and weighs 14 to 15 ounces when ready for play. It is composed of an inflated rubber bladder enclosed in a pebble-grained, brown cowhide case. This exterior is made of top grain leather and has a natural tack to it that makes the ball easier to grip. There is a light protective coating put on the balls at the factory to protect the pebble grain during shipment, which must be rubbed off before the balls are acceptable for play. Since the officiating crew is responsible for the balls, this job is often delegated to the newest member of the officiating crew, and he does it a few hours prior to game time.

13

Timing the Game

A football game has 60 minutes of clocked playing time, unless there is "overtime" (see Glossary), comprised of four 15-minute quarters. An official uses a blank pistol to signal the end of each quarter.

Why, then, does it take over three hours to play a game?

The playing time is kept by the stadium's electric clock, called the "game clock." This is the official clock, and starts with the kickoff to begin the game. It stops at the end of the fourth quarter. In the meantime, it shows the minutes and seconds left to play in each quarter, like 3:59. Even though it times the 12-minute halftime break between the second and third quarters, this is not counted in the overall game time.

The official clock does stop for a number of reasons. Let's look at them:

● **Changing of goals:** One two-minute break comes between the first and second quarters and another between the third and fourth while the teams change goals. This rule goes back to the days when all teams played their games outside and had to contend with the elements. You'd be surprised how much difference it makes to a team whether the wind (or sun) is at its back or face. Even today, more teams play outside than in domed stadiums.

● **Team timeouts:** There can be up to twelve two-minute team timeouts per game. Each team is allowed three per half without a penalty. The referee signals for play to resume after 1 minute and 30 seconds, unless the timeout is in the final two minutes of the half, when it is reduced to 40 seconds. The referee may allow more time for an injured player or repair of equipment.

● **First down measurements:** Whenever a team is close to a first down and it's hard to tell by sight whether the necessary yardage is made, the official calls a timeout, the chain gang officials bring the chain onto the field to the ball, and a measurement is made to see if the pole touches any part of the football. If so, it's a first down, and the referee signals it by pointing toward the goal line of the defending team.

● **Assessment of penalties:** Every time a flag is thrown to denote a foul, the official will stop the clock at the end of the down.   This occurs if the clock is not already stopped as a result of a play such as an incomplete pass. The clock starts again when the ball is declared ready for play.

● **Ball changes possession:** After a kickoff, punt, turnover by interception or fumble, an unsuccessful fourth down, or after a fair catch is made, the clock is stopped.

● **Incompleted passes.**

● **The ball or ball carrier goes out of bounds.**

● **Injuries on the field.**

● **Scoring:** The clock is stopped after a touchdown, field goal, unsuccessful field-goal attempt (unless it's run back) or safety.

● **Two-minute warning:** The referee notifies both head coaches two minutes before the end of the second and fourth quarters of the remaining time.

● **Tackling the quarterback behind the line of scrimmage:** When the quarterback is sacked, or has no intention of advancing the ball, the clock is stopped, giving the quarterback time to get up. The clock starts again as soon as the ball is spotted.

● **Television commercials:** They are planned at predetermined intervals.

● **Throwing pass out of bounds:** A passer may stop the clock by throwing the ball out of bounds or to the ground. To do this, he must start his throwing motion immediately after receiving the snap and throw the ball toward the sideline.

These are examples of official timeouts, and only one is charged to a team as one of its three per half. The obvious exception is the team timeout. A team might use one of its own timeouts to discuss special strategy on the next play, to regroup when confused, to prevent a "delay of game" penalty when the second clock is about to run down or to stop the clock toward the end of a half, when time is of the essence, to score or try and get the ball back.

The Second Clock

Another clock important to the game is the "second clock." It differs from the game clock in that it is used for individual plays. There are identical clocks at each end of the field, and they are located in a prominent place for the players, officials and fans to see. The clocks have large numbers and count down from 45 or 25 seconds. A team is allowed 45 seconds between most plays, except in some circumstances, such as following timeouts, injuries and other usual delays where 25 seconds are allowed.

If a play has not begun by the time the clock runs out, the offense is penalized five yards for "delay of game." These clocks were created because teams used to be able to take as much time as they wanted between downs. The clocks are supposed to speed up play, and they do. It's the large number of timeouts (including commercial timeouts) that causes a game to last so long.

Action Can Go on when Clock is Stopped

Sometimes play goes on when the game clock is off. For example, the clock does not run during PATs. During the last two minutes of the half, the clock does not start on kickoffs until the ball is legally touched by the receiving team in the field of play by a player on the kicking team after the ball has gone ten yards. Normally the clock starts as the ball is kicked.

At the end of a period the clock can run out in the middle of a play, but the period does not end until the play is completed. If the defense commits a foul during the last play of a half, the offense is allowed to run one more play; if a foul by each team occurs during the last play of either half, the period is extended by one down. Similarly, if a kicking team commits a foul during the last play, one more play can be added, even though time has expired. With no time remaining on the clock, teams can still score points; play will continue to be extended if specific fouls are committed.

14

From Coin Toss
to Overtime

This chapter shows an actual football game from coin toss to overtime. I have taken excerpts from an actual radio broadcast, so you're reading it the way announcers talk. I've already given you all the information necessary to understand what's happening. If you don't know something, look it up. You'll remember it longer. Sorry I can't be there with you, but I was at the game you're reading about. You're on your own. Good luck!

Hi again, and welcome, everybody, to our Monday night edition of "Detroit Lions Football," live tonight from the Silverdome. It's the Lions in Chuck Long's starting debut against the world champion Chicago Bears.

Out at the center of the field William Gay and Keith Dorney represent the Lions . . . six Bears captains out there with Referee Pat Haggerty . . . let's tune in on the coin toss:

"Heads!" he calls.

"It's tails."

And so with the tails coming up that means that Chuck Long will open up the ball game with the Lions offense against that vaunted Chicago defense, which is number one in the NFL—allowing opposing quarterbacks to complete only 47 of their passes. The Bears, with 27 interceptions this year, have allowed only ten passing touchdowns, and if that's impressive, consider they've allowed only four touchdowns on the ground, and none since the Lions scored via the ground route seven weeks ago.

So the Lions and Chuck Long will be on the field first, and we'll be back with the Bears' opening kickoff in one minute ...

The opening kick by Kevin Butler taken by Herman Hunter back at the goal line and he heads up the middle .. . cuts to his right ... gets over the 10 ... and back up defensive back Reggie Phillips hauls him down on the 13. And so Chuck Long is forced to start in poor field position.

Here's our starting lineup: Steve Mott at center, the guards are Keith Dorney and Harvey Salem, the tackles for the Lions Rich Strenger and Lomas Brown, Carl Bland and Jeff Chadwick the wide receivers, Jim Giles at tight end, Garry James and James Jones with rookie Chuck Long in the backfield.

I formation—Bears: six men at the line and Long's back to throw ... he's going deep for Chadwick on a post ... slightly underthrown ... Chadwick double-covered and the ball batted away by Vestee Jackson and Gary Fencik. And so the Lions come out with the bomb with Chuck Long on his first play as a starter. He's 0 for 1 as a starter, 1 for 2 on the year.

Bears in that 4-3 defense: Steve McMichael, William Perry the tackles; Dan Hampton and Richard Dent the ends; Mike Singletary, Wilbur Marshall and Otis Wilson the three best linebackers in pro football. Out of the I a handoff: Garry James, left side, busts over the tackle spot and is out to the 20, 23, 24 for 11 yards and a first down before Dave Duerson the safety could come up to make the stop.

That secondary for the Bears: Dave Duerson at strong safety, six interceptions to tie Mike Richardson, the left corner, for team honors; Gary Fencik the free safety; and rookie Vestee Jackson has come on to take over that right corner spot from second year man Reggie Phillips.

First and 10: Lions on the 24 after the 11 yard pick-up by James and here he comes again ... but this time he runs into Hampton, tries to fight forward ... but there's not much room there and Garry James somehow squirms out to the 27 where Perry and McMichael and Singletary help Hampton make the stop. It'll be a pick-up of 3 and will bring up second and 7 for the Lions. The Bears show six men up at the line of scrimmage as Otis Wilson jumps in there . . . now they've got seven, now eight, and Long drops to throw . . . big rush coming from McMichael . . . he throws in the right flat . . . incomplete for Garry James and Long was hit as he delivered the ball by McMichael and Otis Wilson.

This line for the Detroit Lions is going to have to handle that front four, front six sometimes and if they can do that, Chuck Long is going to have the opportunity to play his ball game. This game is going to be won or lost in the trenches.

Long 0 for 2 now, the Lions facing third and 7 from their own 27. Lions go to their Nickel offense. They've got Herman Hunter in that backfield replacing Garry James. They go to three wide receivers with the tight end Giles out, Leonard Thompson in. Thompson split to the right, Chadwick is slot left, Bland wide left. Bears jumping around . . . seven men at the line, back is Long . . . quick snap . . . that ball is caught by Carl Bland over the 45, out to the 46. They got the Bears in that little blitz and Chuck Long delivered it on the slant to Carl Bland for a pick-up of 19 yards and a first down before Vestee, the rookie, could bring him down.

Garry James back in now and out comes Herman Hunter. The Lions with two first downs as Long completes his first pass as a starter to Carl Bland for 19 yards . . . Bland split to the right, Chadwick to the left, the backs in a Power Right and here's a handoff: James Jones springing up the middle . . . fights forward to about the 48 . . . and that's all. Otis Wilson knifed in from that left outside linebacking spot to haul down Jones after a gain of 2. It'll bring up second and 8 for the Lions from their own 48—now the officials mark it up at the 49 so give Jones 3 on the play and call it second and 7.

The Bears have held their last 14 NFC Central opponents to under 100 yards rushing. That dates back to the opener in '85 against the Bucs—you won't see that tonight.

The Lions have 17 yards in three rushing attempts thus far. Again the backs in a Power Right, and here's Long back to throw . . . blitz coming . . . he fires right sideline . . . Chadwick had not made his cut . . . the ball falls incomplete and Long is belted to the ground by Richard

Dent. That'll bring up third down and 7. Chuck seemed to be throwing that one to a spot, too.

Now whether Chadwick was supposed to run a 10-yard or 14-yard made a difference in the completion. Lions 1 out of 1 in third down situations face third down and 7 at their own 49.

Leonard Thompson goes in as a third wide receiver . . . Garry James out of the backfield . . . Herman Hunter is in. There's five defensive backs in: the fifth is Todd Bell and they have nine men up at the line of scrimmage. Long drops to throw . . . big blitz coming . . . he's going to be sacked back at the 40- yard line. He had no chance—Dave Duerson the strong safety was coming and he gets his seventh sack of the season. The Bears just overpowered the offensive line that time. Had too many people up there—the Lions couldn't pick 'em up and it's a loss of 8 yards.

That'll bring up fourth down and in to punt comes Jim Arnold. Going deep for the Bears is Lew Barnes. He's been their only punt returner this year, a rookie fifth-round draft choice out of Oregon. Barnes is averaging some 7.4 yards a return. Eric Sanders snaps it . . . the Bears try to get through but Arnold kicks it away . . . hangs it high . . . good kick toward the far sideline. Barnes calls fair catch . . . lets it bounce inside the 10. It gets into the end zone despite the efforts of Donnie Elder, who was chasing down after it . . . a 59-yard punt . . . the Bears will start on their 20 after a touchback and we've got timeout on the field . . . the Lions nothing, Chicago nothing.

We pause for these words on the Detroit Lions Football network . . . .

Wow! And that's only *one* team possession. It included nine plays and took eight minutes.

If I were to print Frank Beckmann's account of the Bears' first possession, you would see he names their entire offensive unit as well as the Lions' defensive team just as he gave the Lions' offense and Bears' defense in Detroit's first possession. He sets the stage and names the main characters early so you'll recognize them when they appear later. Radio sports announcers are very informative because their description of a game must let you "see" what you're listening to.

Since a game averages 130 plays and lasts about three-and-a- half hours, reproducing a broadcast of an entire game would require too much space and take too long to read. So I've compromised: I'm pushing the fast forward button and giving you an account of the game in abbreviated form.

Before I start, however, I would like to mention a couple of things. First, for ease of reading I've used only the names of those players who appear most frequently, but if you're going to be a fan, it's important to learn more names than just those of the stars:

> quarterbacks:
> > Chicago—Doug Flutie
> > Detroit—Chuck Long

> place-kickers:
> > Chicago—Kevin Butler
> > Detroit—Eddie Murray

> punters:
> > Chicago—Maury Buford
> > Detroit—Jim Arnold

Second, when I refer to "plays" (and there were 140 in this game), they include running, passing and kicking. In many, I do not say which one was used unless it was per--tinent to the game.

So we continue the game with the Bears in possession of the ball following Detroit's receiving the game kick-off, having two first downs but not being able to score in eight plays and having to punt.

When the Bears took over they had six plays before punting on fourth and 4 from their 40. The Lions lost a couple yards on the return and took over on their own 18. They ran six plays before facing a fourth down and 3 from the Bears' 34. Eddie Murray, the Lions' place-kicker, came in and kicked a 52-yard field goal—his longest ever—with 4:09 left in the first quarter.

Detroit 3, Chicago 0.

The Bears' deep man took Murray's kickoff from two yards in the Bears' end zone and ran it back to their 29. They ran eight plays before time ran out in the first quarter and the teams changed fields.

The Second Quarter

After beginning the second quarter, Chicago was penalized for a false start on the second play and illegal motion on the third. The Lions declined the illegal motion penalty. That brought up fourth and 11 on the Lions 25, so the Bears brought in their place-kicker, Maury Buford, to attempt a field goal. Detroit had 11 men on the line, but the 42-yarder was successful with 12:39 remaining in the half. It was now Detroit 3, Chicago 3.

The Lions took the kickoff after the field goal on the 1 and ran it back to their 17. On the first play they had an offensive holding and the penalty was half the distance to the goal. They weren't able to get a first down so they punted. The Bears' special teams put ten defensive men on the line and partially blocked the kick, so the ball stopped on Detroit's 45. Good field position for Chicago.

The Bears' first play was an incompleted pass, but the Lions roughed the passer for a 15-yard penalty. On the next play, a Lion intercepted a Flutie pass, was hit and fumbled the ball, but it was recovered by another Lion who ran 27 yards with it. The officials ruled that the ground caused the fumble and moved the ball back to the spot where the fumble occurred. But it was still Detroit's ball.

The Lions didn't do much on their offensive possession, and punted after six plays. The ball hit on Chicago's 2, went into the end zone for a touchback, and the Bears took over on their own 20.

They ran seven plays before the referee gave the two-minute warning to the benches. After two more plays, it was fourth down and six on Detroit's 35. Chicago took a timeout to decide what to do. They went for the first down. Flutie was sacked, and Detroit took over.

On Detroit's next possession, Chicago was penalized three times—five yards for inadvertently grabbing a face mask, five for offside, and then half the distance to the goal line for roughing the passer, Chuck Long. The Lions ran nine plays with two quarterback sacks, and had a fourth down on the Bears' 22 when Murray successfully kicked a 39-yard field goal. With 15 seconds remaining in the first half, the Lions took the lead over the Bears by a score of 6-3.

On Murray's ensuing kickoff, the ball went 4 yards deep into the end zone. The receiver thought about running it out but stayed in and went down on one knee for a touchback. On the first play from its 20, Chicago had an ineligible receiver downfield and was penalized 10 yards. On the next play, the quarterback received the snap and went down as time ran out in the first half.

Halftime

During halftime, the teams go to their respective locker rooms, review what happened in the first half and try to make any necessary adjustments in the game plan for the second half. As a fan you have several options as the stadium clock ticks off 12 minutes. You can discuss the first half with a friend, or enjoy the band or any other planned activity on the field. What about standing up and stretching, or maybe even edging your way (remember, no pushing or illegal use of hands) to a munchie stand? Diets are meant to be ignored at ball games.

It's time to settle down when the teams come back on the field with about a minute left in the halftime. The punters and place- kickers practice a few kicks.

Since the Lions won the opening coin toss and elected to receive the kickoff, the referee indicated that the Bears chose to receive the kickoff in the second half.

The Second Half

Here we go.

The teams lined up on the field and Murray kicked the ball to the Bears' deep man, who caught the ball on his 7 and was finally hauled down on the 18. On the next play, the Bears fumbled and the Lions recovered on Chicago's 11-yard line.

On the second play Detroit fumbled, the Bears recovered the ball and took over on their own 23.

Before the third down began, the 30-second clock ran down and Chicago was penalized 5 yards for taking too much time. On the next down, Buford punted 57 yards, his second longest of the season.

The Lions took over. On the third down the Bears were penalized 15 yards for a personal foul—kicking a player—but came back and intercepted a pass two plays later.

Flutie was sacked on the third play and Buford punted a 42- yarder on the fourth down.

Detroit was not able to get a first down on its next possession, so it punted on fourth down, and Arnold punted his longest as a Lion—60 yards—and his team-mates downed the ball on Chicago's 1-yard line. So the Bears had 99 yards to go for a touchdown.

Payton fumbled on the first play and Detroit recovered, so with first and goal on the 4, Long lofted the ball to Thompson in the end zone for a touchdown. Murray came in and kicked the point-after touchdown.

It was then the Lions 13, Bears 3.

Murray's kickoff was taken on the 8 and returned to the 29. Detroit came with six defensive backs, four line-men and one linebacker. After half a dozen plays, the Bears' Buford punted on fourth down from his own 45. The ball traveled 55 yards and bounced into the end zone for a touchback.

On Detroit's second and long, the blitz was on after Long called an audible. Before the next down he called a timeout to clarify the plays being sent in. He was sacked on the next play and Arnold punted on fourth and 9 from the Lions' 21.

The Bears' receiver took the ball for a 54-yard return with Arnold finally bringing down the runner. However, Chicago fumbled at their own 23 on the second play—their third fumble of the game.

Long threw a long pass that would have been a touchdown if it had not been underthrown, because his receiver was in the open. Before the third down started, Detroit took too much time getting the ball away and was penalized 5 yards for delay of game. With ten seconds left in the quarter, the Lions let the clock run down; so at the end of three quarters it was Lions 13, Bears 3.

The Fourth Quarter

On the opening play of the fourth quarter, Arnold kicked a 40- yard punt, but the receiver broke tackle for a 21-yard return and good field position on the Lions' 40.

On the second play, the flag was thrown for a personal foul against Detroit—unnecessary roughness. The Bears took a timeout and on the next play had a false start, followed by two incomplete passes. So on fourth and 11 Buford kicked a 32-yard field goal. With 12:26 remaining in the game, the score was Detroit 13, Chicago 6.

Up until now in the second half the Lions had four first downs and the Bears two.

Butler's line drive kickoff hit on the 5, bounced high, and went 2 yards deep into the end zone, but the deep man chose to run it out and got to the 17. Long was sacked for a fourth time on the second down, and on fourth and 4 Arnold punted 52 yards.

In the next eight plays, the Bears advanced 74 yards for a touchdown. Butler kicked the point-after touchdown, so with 5:49 left to go in the ball game, the score was Detroit 13, Chicago 13.

Butler booted the kickoff high and deep—a yard into the end zone. Detroit's receiver decided to run it out and was tackled on the 16.

The Bears quickly got the ball back on their own 45, and after an incompleted pass, earned two first downs on gains of 17, 9 and 8. With second and 3 on the Lions' 17, the two minute warning was given. Each team had two timeouts remaining.

After the next play, it was necessary to bring the chain in to measure for a first down. The ball was a few inches shy, but the Bears made it on the next try and then moved the ball another 4 yards to the 10. On second down at the 10, with 43 seconds left, the Lions took their second timeout.

On third and 4 at the 8, with 38 seconds remaining, the Lions called their third timeout. Then on fourth and 1 at the 5, the Bears let the clock run down to four seconds and took a timeout.

Butler came in and kicked a successful field goal from 22 yards away as the clock ran out. Final score: the Chicago Bears 16, the Detroit Lions 13.

You've just been to an entire football game. It might not have been terribly exciting to read, but I can tell you it sure was thrilling to watch. *Nothing* takes the place of live action. Reading about it, however, gave you an opportunity to see what happens at a real game, and it sounded familiar, didn't it? Do you know why? Because for the first time ever, perhaps, you understood it. Football lingo is no longer a foreign language to you. Isn't it amazing the difference a little knowledge makes?

Overtime

One more thing: I promised you overtime, so we're going to play "what if." What if the Bears had missed the field goal and the game ended in a 13-13 tie?

There would have been a sudden death overtime. Before overtime begins the team captains come with the referee to the middle of the field for the coin toss, with the same rules as the pre-game toss. There is a three-minute intermission.

Each team gets two timeouts. Play begins with a kickoff and continues for 15 minutes or until there is a score. The team scoring first during overtime play is the winner and the game automatically ends upon any score—touchdown, field goal, or safety. If there is no score after 15 minutes of play, the game remains a tie and is over.

This holds true for pre-season and regular season games. Post- season playoff games cannot end in a tie: so 15-minute periods continue until there is a score and a winner. Each team gets three timeouts, and there are two-minute intermissions between each period as the teams change fields.

So now you know what happens in an average game and one that ends in a tie. What else is there to know?

15

Personnel Behind the Scenes

You can't have a football team without players, but for every player there are several helpers behind the scenes. A football game is like a stage play. It cannot be produced without actors, financial backing, set and costume designers, and a host of other people all working behind the scenes. On a football team these people are the trainers, coaches and managers. This chapter explains who these people are and what they do.

The Management

Every pro team has an owner, or a group of investors, who finances all the expenses of fielding a team. This includes salaries, equipment and travel. Some revenue is brought in from tickets, TV rights and sometimes concessions, but it is the owner who is ultimately responsible for paying the bills.

A typical management staff includes the president, who is usually the owner or one of the owners, the executive vice president, the general manager, the secretary-legal counsel, the treasurer and the head coach.

Football Organization

The people directly responsible for putting a team on the field are the coaching staff, the equipment manager, and the head trainer, plus assistants. Hundreds of other people are necessary for a game, like security and parking personnel, ushers, ticket takers and concessions staff. There are team doctors, a travel coordinator, ticket manager and many others essential to team management. These include player and scouting personnel, public relations staff, controller, video director and computer coordinator. In addition, there is a game-day crew of photographers and persons responsible for field activities—the press box, public address and statistics. Each special job is vital for smooth team operations.

Coaching Staff

The staff we're most familiar with is the coaching staff. Quite often the head coach also has the title of director of football operations, which means he is responsible not only for his coaches and players but also player procurement, college draft and free agents.

A typical coaching staff includes about 12 people. Besides the head coach, there is an offensive coordinator who, in addition to being responsible for the quarterbacks, oversees the offensive coaches who work with the running backs, receivers, tight ends, and linemen. The coaches in charge of the defensive backs, linebackers, defensive line and special teams are accountable to the defensive coordinator.

Frequently the coaches are blamed for a team's not doing well, even though a change in coaches does not guarantee a change in a team's fortunes. Although the plays may look unimaginative and predictable, a game plan is carefully mapped out according to the players' capabilities. Speaking of mapping out game plans, the computer is indispensable. It is used for everything from rating and drafting college players to analyzing opponents and planning game strategies. But the best laid plans often go awry. Since human beings have the job of carrying these strategies out, mistakes are sometimes made.

Some spectators analyze every play. Second guessing is a great sport for everybody except the coaches, who have to guess right the first time. You think *you* feel bad when you see a player on your team drop an "easy" pass or miss an "easy" tackle? Think how the coach feels who works with the player every day in practice.

The coaches work year around with about two weeks off. In the off-season they evaluate personnel, study game tapes from previous seasons, revise plays and review the college prospects in the upcoming draft. They have an

especially busy schedule during the football season, when
they work seven days a week for six months.

A Typical Week at the Office

What is a typical mid-season week like for the
coaching staff? On a game-day part of the coaching staff
is on the sidelines while others work in the upper deck
watching, and filming the action below.

After a Sunday game, the coaching staff views game
film. On Monday morning they analyze the film carefully by looking at each play and every player involved in
each play to try and determine what was done right or
wrong.

Then comes the inquest.

In the afternoon, the players assemble at the stadium
to view the previous day's game in slow motion. Then
they break up into groups according to position played
and watch the game bit by bit so no error goes unnoticed. There's no rock to hide under. Well, after a royal
"chewing out" (remember, this book is PG-rated) and
much embarrassment over missed tackles and dropped
passes, the session is over. Kaput.

Tuesday is the players' day for rest and relaxation.
Coaches spend their Tuesdays reviewing their next opponent's films, looking for strengths and weaknesses and
devising a game plan they think will give them the best
chance for a win.

Wednesday, Thursday, Friday (and sometimes part of
Saturday if it's a home game) are practice days. During
this time each coach works with his own group of players. For example, the defensive backfield coach would be
with the cornerbacks and safeties, and the offensive line
coach with the interior linemen—centers, tackles and
guards.

After this intensive week you may think Saturday night
is party time, right? Wrong. There is a strict curfew with
heavy fines for noncompliance. Some of us remember
college days (back in the Stone Ages) when girls had to
be in their all-female dorms by midnight on the weekend.
It's the same thing with football teams.

Sunday morning arrives with complete optimism. At
kickoff time both teams are equal and on any given
Sunday any NFL can beat any other one.

Job Security

Just as the saying "it's not easy being green" goes, it's not easy being a coach, either, whether it's head or assistant coach. You get flak either way. You've got a job as long as you produce, and you can only produce if your players do. To be a coach, you really have to love the game because it's not famous for its job security.

Why not job security? A head coach hires assistants who will carry out his philosophy; so, when a head coach is released, most of his assistants are also. Sometimes it takes a while to find another coach and team who can use them.

Besides the love of football, what are the other job requirements of a coach? Mainly, a thorough knowledge of the game and the ability to get along with people.

What are the chances of an assistant becoming a head coach in the NFL? Just like the game officials, where many start in Little League or junior high and work their way up, most assistants put in 15 to 20 years before their status and age make them head coach material. Many never get the chance. It's a career that requires timing as much as skill. Being with a winning franchise certainly could accelerate a head coaching possibility, but not all assistants have the same desire or potential to be a head coach. Some don't want the pressure, while others realize they aren't head coaching material—even though their salary could rise four times higher.

The Trainer and Equipment Manager

Two other employees are indispensable for fielding a team: the trainer and the equipment manager. What are the requirements for their jobs?

I'll start with the equipment manager, since I told you about him and his importance in Chapter 12, but I didn't say how he got the position. On-the-job training is the most important requirement, with a few years as an understudy in order to learn the business. There are college courses in sports management, but they're not required. Equipment managers must find their work enjoyable and rewarding, because they tend to remain with a team even though coaches come and go. The former equipment manager for the Detroit Lions was with the team for 45 years. The present one, Dan Jaroshewich, is in his 18th year and only in his mid-thirties. Jaroshewich has completed college and taken graduate work in sports administration during his tenure.

What are the qualifications of a trainer? To be an athletic trainer, a person must have a college degree with certain course requirements and a minimum number of supervised hours in a training room. Then, to be certified (A.T.,C.), it is necessary to take a three part test—oral, written and practical. Although certification never used to be required in order to be an athletic trainer, Kent Falb, who is an A.T.,C. and has been with the Detroit Lions 24 years, says, "It is virtually mandatory in applying for a job, especially when trainers' jobs are a premium." The NFL now requires newly hired trainers to be certified.

A team could not function without a qualified training staff. Falb of the Lions has a full-time assistant and a part-time assistant to help him tape the players prior to each practice and game. The amount of bandaging depends on the players' present and past injuries and the position they play. For example, linemen have more taping than a wide receiver because every play for them involves physical contact.

Who determines whether or not a player is physically able to play in a game? Professional football is a business, and unfortunately it's the only way some players know of earning a living. They realize if they're not able to play, someone will replace them—temporarily at first, but eventually for good. The game goes on without a player, no matter how good he is, so most learn to play with pain. When Dr. Robert Teitge was the Detroit Lions' team doctor, he was asked how much pain a typical player had the day after a game. He responded, "Quite a bit. For half of them, their injuries are to the extent that, if they were an average person the pain would prompt them to see a physician."

Frequently, a player says he feels fine and wants to play even though he looks like the loser in a fight against Rocky Balboa, while another player might have no visible wounds and say he hurts. By acute observation and proper therapy, a trainer can often make the difference in the number of years a player is physically able to play football.

The players are checked after each game. Sometimes it's hard to tell an injury from all the aches, pains, bruises and muscle strains. The trainer works with the team doctors and is the liaison between them and the players. The doctors have the final say as to whether or not a player is in condition to practice and/or play, and what treatment is to be used in the training room.

The head trainer is the first staff person on the field when an injured player is down. He asks what's wrong, and depending on the response or non-response, he determines whether he needs his assistant and/or the team doctor and what equipment, like a stretcher, might be required.

The training staff works year around to supervise not only the rehabilitation of players after injuries, but also the weight room training to keep as many players as possible in top physical condition. The fewer and least severe the number of injuries, the more longevity to a player's career.

16

National Football League

How can a team with an 8-8 record make the playoffs while a team with an 11-5 record doesn't? To understand how such an apparently absurd situation can happen you have to understand the way that the National Football League (NFL) is organized.

The National Football League, a nonprofit association of the 28 team owners, is headquartered in New York under the supervision of a team owner-elected Commissioner. The NFL oversees all aspects of the game except the team's personnel, which is a franchise's responsibility. The owners, known as the Management Council, elect an Executive Director to represent them. They meet periodically during the year to discuss the events of the previous year, possible rule changes and the NFL's operation.

The NFL teams are divided into two conferences, the American and the National, which are primarily based on whichever leagues the teams originally started with. A short history of pro football in the United States may help you understand these origins.

A Brief History of the NFL

Professional football has come a long way from pro games in 1895, when a player received ten dollars per game. Play was poorly organized then, and there were few fans.

The American Professional Football Association was formed in 1920 when George Halas, father of the National Football League, begged 12 other men to throw $100 into a pot in Canton, Ohio. Within two years a player's contract was worth $50 and the APFA changed its name to the National Football League (NFL). Halas (Papa Bear, as he was known) is credited with bringing the NFL out of its infancy after taking his Chicago Bears and newly- signed player Red Grange on a 16-game cross-country tour in 1925.

Two divisions were set up in 1933, and the annual drafting of college players began two years later. Still, it wasn't until the 1950s that professional football became popular in the United States and started attracting large numbers of followers. The advent of television spread the popularity of pro football.

The American Football League (AFL) was organized in 1959, and merged with the NFL in 1966. It created two conferences and played the first championship game in 1967. This annual contest became known as the Super Bowl in 1971. With some exceptions, the former NFL teams became known as the NFC (National Football Conference) and the earlier AFL teams became the AFC (American Football Conference). The current divisional arrangement came in 1970. Three teams have since moved but remain in their same division: the Baltimore Colts have become the Indianapolis Colts, the Oakland Raiders have become the Los Angeles Raiders and the St. Louis Cardinals have become the Phoenix Cardinals.

You may be surprised to know the NFL seems to have an influence on the stock market. It's uncanny, but the Super Bowl has been one of the most reliable stock market predictors since the first game. With only two minor exceptions, the market went up in years when the winner was a team that was, or used to be, in the NFC.

Road to the Super Bowl

Now you know what the NFL is, but what is the Super Bowl? It's a football game that has become an international spectacle. The 1987 contest was beamed by satellite to over 60 countries including the Peoples' Republic of China. The media interest has mushroomed from 200 sportswriters in 1967 to 2,000 in 1987. The Super Bowl championship is the goal of every NFL team. The game is played between the NFC and the AFC champions in January, about a month after the season ends. The weeks in between are used for the playoffs.

National Football League

The National Football Conference

Eastern Division	Central Division	Western Division
Dallas Cowboys	Chicago Bears	Atlanta Falcons
New York Giants	Detroit Lions	Los Angeles Rams
Philadelphia Eagles	Green Bay Packers	New Orleans Saints
Phoenix Cardinals	Minnesota Vikings	San Francisco '49ers
Washington Redskins	Tampa Bay Buccaneers	

The American Football Conference

Eastern Division	Central Division	Western Division
Buffalo Bills	Cincinnati Bengals	Denver Broncos
Indianapolis Colts	Cleveland Browns	Kansas City Chiefs
Miami Dolphins	Houston Oilers	Los Angeles Raiders
New England Patriots	Pittsburgh Steelers	San Diego Chargers
New York Jets		Seattle Seahawks

You're probably asking what the big deal is about winning a divisional or conference title. The players of each team making the single elimination playoffs receive a bonus for each post-season game they play in. The January 1990 Super Bowl game was worth an extra $36,000 to each of the winning players, and $18,000 to the losing ones. Not bad for 60 minutes of doing what you enjoy, eh?

Of the 28 teams in the NFL, 14 are in each conference, and each conference is made up of three divisions. They are listed on page 130. You can also find them in the sports section of major newspapers during the football season.

Summer training camp officially begins two weeks prior to a team's first scheduled pre-season game. Quarterbacks, rookies and injured players may be required to report earlier.

Early in August, the annual Pro Football Hall of Fame game is played between two different teams in Canton, Ohio. The game and the festivities are intended to honor the inductees—retired players and other contributors to the game of football—who are elected by a national board.

In order to give other countries a chance to watch American football live, the NFl sponsored the first American Bowl game in 1986 at Wembley Arena in London. International interest continues to develop, in part because of the annual exhibition games played abroad.

The league plays a 20-game season from August to January. The first four games are considered "pre-season" or "exhibition." Teams are allowed to begin with a limited number of players but must pare their rosters in a series of required reductions before the season opener. The pre-season games do not count in the standings or individual records, but the final 16 games, when teams are permitted to dress up to 45 players, do count.

Each team plays two games—home and away—against all other teams in its division, and the rest of the 16-game schedule is based on a common-opponent formula that uses the team's division standing from the prior season. This is to give the teams a competitive format with evenly matched opponents.

Half of each team's games are played on its home field, the other half on the opponents' fields. Each team's goal for the year is to achieve a record good enough to qualify for the post-season playoffs, ultimately leading to the Super Bowl.

At the end of the season the team with the best won-lost-tied record in its division is the division champion. In case of a tie, the NFL has steps to break it. There are variations in the formula, but basically the tied teams are compared according to the following criteria:

1. with one another (best won-lost-tied percentage)
2. won-lost-tied games within the division
3. won-lost-tied games within the conference
4. common games (this means comparing how the teams did against the same opponents)
5. best net points in division games
6. best net points in all games
7. strength of schedule (how well rated the teams were on their schedule—first place or last)
8. best net touchdowns in all games
9. a coin toss

Each of the six divisions will produce one division champion, three in each conference. Three teams in each conference with the best records, who were not divisional winners, are wild card teams. Ties for wild cards are broken in a manner that varies slightly from the one mentioned above. Step two is eliminated if the tied teams are not in the same division. Also, step five is changed from best net points in division games (unless tied teams are in the same division) to best average net points in conference games. So now there are six teams—three divisional champions and three wild cards—in each conference to begin the playoffs. These begin the week after the regular season ends. Each game is played on the field of the team with the better season record. This is known as "home field advantage," because teams tend to win more games on their own field due to the home town crowds cheering for them.

Wild Card Teams

During the first week of the playoffs, the two division champions with the best records get byes and do not play. The remaining division champion plays the wild-card with the third best record, and the other two wild-card teams play each other. The second week, the two first-round winners play the two division champions who drew byes in the first round. The third week, the two second-round winners play for the conference championship. Finally, in round four, the conference champions compete in the Super Bowl for the NFL Championship and the Vince Lombardi trophy.

To make it easier to understand, I've summarized the playoff schedule below. Both conferences follow the same playoff procedure.

First week—third-best division champion versus the third-best wild-card; first-best wild-card against the second-best wild- card;

Second week—team with best record of the division winners versus the wild card winner from round one with worst record; team with second-best record of the division winners against other winner of round one;

Third week—winners of second-week game for conference championship;

Fourth Week (Super Bowl)—winner of third-week game in NFC against the winner of third-week game in AFC.

The season ends with the Pro Bowl, the week after the Super Bowl. This game is played by the best NFC players against the best from the AFC, as chosen by their peers and coaches. All elected players participate, and the expenses for the players and their families are paid by the NFL in appreciation for an outstanding season.

I know it sounds complicated, but as the football season winds down and you hear about divisional winners,

wild card playoffs and the Super Bowl, you can refer to
this chapter to understand what's happening.

17

College Football

The most exuberant football crowds are found at college games. New attendance records show the number of people attending games is at an all-time high. In 1986, eight schools averaged more in attendance than any NFL team. At least four major colleges average 90,000 people at each of their five or six home contests every season. The University of Michigan has been the country's all-time leader for nearly a decade and a half, averaging more than 104,000 fans per home game. Just think how many spectators there are each weekend during football season when there are over 650 men's intercollegiate varsity teams. Over three million!

We've learned about the NFL's authority over the 28 professional teams, but there are nearly 24 times as many collegiate teams. How can they possibly be monitored and controlled?

Roots of College Football

Intercollegiate football celebrated its 100th birthday in 1969. A century earlier, Princeton and Rutgers played the first game between colleges. The beginning of football as we know it today, however, is attributed to a two-game series in 1874 between McGill University of Montreal and Harvard. One game was played with Canadian rugby rules, where a player could run with the ball and throw it. The other game used U.S. soccer rules that allowed players only to kick the ball. Harvard liked the new running game and introduced it to Yale the next year. Thus, the combination of both rules came about.

Harvard and McGill joined Princeton, Rutgers and Columbia in 1876 to form the first collegiate league and then the game began to grow. College football began as a disorganized sport until the Intercollegiate Athletic Association of United States (IAAUS) was formed in 1906. It changed its name to National Collegiate Athletic Association (NCAA) in 1910. The association was formed for the purpose of regulating athletics at the college level. Its duties include establishing recruiting standards and eligibility of players, formulating rules and seeing they're followed, keeping records and conducting championship competition at the end of the season. The NCAA meets annually to review existing rules and decide if any changes should be made, and to hear complaints and other comments a member representative might bring up for discussion.

The National Association of Intercollegiate Athletics (NAIA) was set up for small colleges and has the same jurisdiction as the NCAA over its members. A number of colleges and universities belong to both. There is a similar group for junior colleges—the National Junior College Athletic Association (NJCAA).

With approximately 15,000 college seniors playing football each year, fewer than 200 succeed in the NFL, so all must train and qualify themselves to make a living at something other than football. With this is mind, the NCAA now requires a minimum grade point average in 11 core courses like English, math, history and science, and a minimum score on the Scholastic Aptitude Test (SAT) before a high school senior can play college ball.

Recruiting

Drafting recruiting rules is another function of the NCAA. Most outstanding high school football players are sought after by several colleges. How, then, does a player choose the "right" one? The college scouts attend high school games, playoffs and state championships and look at films of the exceptional seniors. Speed is a must. A 4.40—running 40 yards in 4.4 seconds—is to a football player what beauty is to a Miss America aspirant. The coaches assess each senior and the positions on the college team that need to be filled due to graduation and/or injuries. They make a priority list and then meet with each player they want, and usually his parents, to explain what the school can offer the young man.

Academics are supposed to be stressed first, before the football program, along with a guarantee of a specific amount of financial aid (scholarship). A prospect will also want to know what his chances are of playing as a freshman. When he decides which school is "right," he signs a "national letter of intent," which is a commitment to attend that school. If an athlete breaks his commitment and attends another college, he cannot play football for the next year and also loses one season of eligibility; so it's important for a high school senior to give serious consideration to all offers before deciding on the college he will attend.

Eligibility to Play

Maintaining player eligibility rules is another function of the NCAA. A player is allowed four seasons of play and must use them within five years. If he is injured and does not play an entire season, or if a coach chooses to postpone any one of his playing seasons, he is "redshirted." That means he has not used one of his four seasons of eligibility. If he is hurt before 20 per cent of the scheduled games have been played and must sit out the rest of the season, he is on "hardship" and is awarded an extra year of eligibility.

From College to Pro Football

The NCAA has no authority over the annual drafting of collegiate players into professional football (see Chapter Five). The NFL has set its own standards, and used to maintain a policy of not drafting a prospective NFL player before he had completed college eligibility or before the year his class graduated. This was to keep a player from going pro before he'd had an opportunity to graduate. However, the NFL now allows players younger than seniors to enter the draft.

Conferences

Colleges organized many conferences to which eight to ten schools typically belong. Most conferences are regionally based, such as the Ivy League Conference in the east, the Big Ten in the midwest and the Pacific Ten on the west coast. Most televised college football games include only the largest schools in the major conferences. A few exceptions are the well-known independent teams, including Notre Dame and University of Miami. The major college football conferences and their teams are listed below.

Atlantic Coast Conference (ACC)

Clemson
Duke
Georgia Tech
North Carolina State University
University of Maryland
University of North Carolina
University of Virginia
Wake Forest

Big Eight Conference

Iowa State University
Kansas State University
Oklahoma State University
University of Colorado
University of Kansas
University of Missouri
University of Nebraska
University of Oklahoma

Big Ten (plus one) Conference

Indiana University
Michigan State University
Northwestern University
Ohio State University

Penn State University
Purdue University
University of Illinois
University of Iowa
University of Michigan
University of Minnesota
University of Wisconsin

Ivy League

Brown University
Columbia University
Cornell University
Dartmouth College
Harvard University
Princeton University
University of Pennsylvania
Yale University

Pacific Ten Conference (PAC-10)

Arizona State University
Stanford University
Oregon State University
University of Arizona
University of California at Berkeley
University of California at Los Angeles (UCLA)
University of Oregon
University of Southern California
University of Washington
Washington State University

Southeastern Conference

Auburn
Louisiana State University (LSU)
Mississippi State University
University of Alabama
University of Florida
University of Georgia
University of Kentucky
University of Mississippi
University of Tennessee
Vanderbilt

Southwest Athletic Conference

Baylor University
Rice University
Southern Methodist University (SMU)
Texas A&M University
Texas Christian University (TCU)
Texas Tech
University of Arkansas
University of Houston
University of Texas

Bowl Games

The first bowl game was the Rose Bowl in 1902 between the University of Michigan (49) and Stanford (0). The major bowls are post-season games for Division I-A schools and are "by invitation only." Each bowl committee sets the requirements and invites prospective teams. Sometimes a team has two or three invitations. The Rose Bowl has not varied since 1947. It has a lock-in arrangement between the Big Ten champion and the winner of the PAC-l0. There are now 19 bowl games, and they're typically played from the middle of December through New Year's Day. The first exception was the 1987 Fiesta Bowl. It was played on January 2 to enable a large TV audience to see the game between the number one and number two ranked teams in the country. Even though there is no playoff game for a I-A national title as yet (the NCAA is considering a I-A national championship game), this was deemed by the pollsters to be the championship game.

You're probably wondering who these pollsters are. The top two polls are published by the Associated Press (sportswriters) and the United Press International Board of Coaches. Both of them rank the top 20 teams each week from pre-season to post-bowl. The AP uses total points based on 20 (most) to 1 (least), while the UPI gives 15 points for first place, 14 for second, etc.

The NCAA does conduct post-season playoffs for a national championship in Divisions l-AA, II and III. These divisions start regional playoffs the last part of November and have their championship game the middle of December—just as do the two divisions in the NAIA.

Rule Differences Between College and the Pros

The are several major differences between college football and NFL football. Although the games appear very similar, a two-point conversion after a touchdown is an option in college football. After a touchdown in college play the scoring team lines up at the 3-yard line (in the NFL, teams line up at the 2-yard line). College teams can kick a PAT for one point or attempt to run or pass the football over the goal line for a two-point conversion. Also on a PAT, collegiate defensemen can score a two-point defensive conversion (see Chapter 4).

You will also notice that the hashmarks in college ball are closer to the sidelines.

In NCAA football games different rules apply to timing the contests. The clock stops when first downs are earned and a 25-second clock is used. In addition, no two-minute warnings are given.

Penalties differ very little between college football and the NFL. However, one significant difference: the penalty for defensive pass interference is 15 yards from the previous line of scrimmage, instead of the spot of the foul. If it's less than 15 yards to the goal, the ball is placed at the spot of the foul. In either case, it's still an automatic first down for the offense, just like the NFL.

The quarterback is an eligible receiver in college football. In the pros he is eligible only when in the shotgun formation. In college play only one foot needs to be in bounds for a pass to be complete. A ball carrier is down if any part of his body, other than his feet or a hand touches the ground. A kickoff out of bounds along the sidelines is rekicked with a 5-yard penalty. These are the major differences.

Remember the most important difference is the option of going for a two-point conversion after touchdowns. This difference changes strategy and eliminates some tie games.

Awards and Trophies

All fall we hear the question, "Who's going to be the Heisman Trophy winner?" Here's what it's all about. John William Heisman coached at eight colleges for a 36-year period in the early 1900s. Even though he will not go down in history as one of the winningest coaches, he was responsible for four innovations in football—the center snap, the hidden ball play, the word "hike" as a vocal sign to start a play and the forward pass. During Heisman's coaching years, Walter Camp, known as the "Father of American Football" because of his long-time association and contributions to the NCAA Rules Committee, had been picking an annual list of the 11 players who were the best in their position. That's when players played "both ways"—offense and defense. Ten years after Camp died it was suggested to modify his idea by selecting one player each year as "the best college football player in the nation." The sportswriters do the voting, and the award is named in honor of Heisman for all his contributions. In 1935, the first award ceremony was held at the New York Athletic Club, and the John N. Heisman Memorial Trophy was presented. Most of the time it has gone to a running back but in recent years it has been awarded to several quarterbacks.

There are other awards but none is as prestigious. There is the Butkus Award given to the best linebacker, the Lombardi to the best lineman, and the Outland to the best interior lineman. The Walter Camp and Maxwell trophies are presented to exceptional players at any position.

All-American teams are selected each year by various newspapers, magazines and news services. In addition, all-star bowl games follow the holiday bowls. Besides collecting money to aid charities, these games are held primarily to reward some of college's best senior players with a nice trip and a final chance to impress professional scouts.

NCAA Certified Post-Season Football Bowl Games

All American Bowl
Birmingham, Alabama
At-large teams (selected by Bowl Committee)

Aloha Bowl
Honolulu, Hawaii
At-Large teams

Copper Bowl
Tucson, Arizona
At-large teams

California Raisin Bowl
Fresno, California
Pacific Coast Athletic Association champion
vs.
Mid-American Athletic Association champion

Cotton Bowl
Dallas, Texas
Southwest Athletic Conference champion
vs.
At-large team

Sunkist Fiesta Bowl
Phoenix, Arizona
At-Large teams

Florida Citrus Bowl
Orlando, Florida
At-large teams

Freedom Bowl
Anaheim, California
At-large teams

Gator Bowl
Jacksonville, Florida
At-large teams

Hall of Fame Bowl
Tampa, Florida

At-large teams

Holiday Bowl
San Diego, California
At-large teams

Independence Bowl
Shreveport, Louisiana
At-large teams

Liberty Bowl
Memphis, Tennessee
At-large teams

Orange Bowl
Miami, Florida
Big Eight Conference champion
vs.
At-large team

Peach Bowl
Atlanta, Georgia
At-large teams

Rose Bowl
Los Angeles, California
Pacific Ten Conference champion
vs.
Big Ten Conference champion

Sugar Bowl
New Orleans, Louisiana
Southeastern Conference champion
vs.
At-large team

John Hancock Bowl
El Paso, Texas
At-large teams

Sunshine Bowl
Hollywood, Florida
At-large teams

18

High School Football

High school football looks very different from college and pro football, partly because of the uneven skills of the players. You will see mostly running plays in high school, a few more passing plays in college and a more balanced attack in the NFL. The rules of high school football vary in different areas, while college and pro rules are uniform throughout the country.

High school football builds the foundation for college and professional football. The top high school players hope to play college or professional football some day. Coaches work all year, sometimes many years, and hope for the time when talent, teamwork and luck all come together to earn the team the ultimate in high school football—the state championship.

If you know someone who plays high school football, you've probably attended some of his games and maybe even a state championship. They're really exciting and they're also a bargain—in Michigan, for example, you can see two state title games for five dollars. Most importantly, you'll see future college and NFL players.

Not Banned in Boston

The first football contest between secondary schools was held in Boston in 1860, after being banned across the Charles River in Cambridge at Harvard. The rules were loose and varied but by the turn of the century, much progress had been made not only toward uniformity, but safety as well.

Safety Considerations

Every year we hear about serious injuries during high school football games. With more than 500,000 high school football players competing every year, injuries are inevitable. These injuries happen because the size and talent of high school players vary considerably. Also, in high school many players play both offense and defense. High school coaches are often faced with a few outstanding players who they try to utilize the most. Teenage boys think that they have enough energy and stamina to play both offense and defense, but exhaustion and more serious injuries can result when a player is extended beyond reasonable limits. Considerable strides have been made to improve equipment to reduce the seriousness and quantity of injuries.

The National Federation of State High School Associations wrote the first high school football rules in 1930, partly to make football safer for high school players. The NFSHSA realizes that rules and their enforcement alone will not make football safe, that equipment as well is essential. Safety standards for helmets are especially important since most football fatalities are the result of head injuries. The National Federation rules require all players to be equipped with helmets with the seal of the National Operating Committee on Standards for Athletic Equipment (NOCSAE). This group was formed in response to a need for a safety standard for football helmets. After extensive study and experimentation it began certifying helmets in 1975. It also conducts tests on other athletic equipment.

More than 12,650 high schools conform to the rules set by the NFSHSA through a committee with a representative from each member state. Besides the rules, the NFSHSA makes a recommendation for overtime sessions, but leaves the final decision up to each state athletic association.

It is up to each state athletic association to decide the criteria for classifying its schools, eligibility of players, interpreting and upholding the rules established by the Federation. In addition these associations organize state playoffs and championship games at the end of the season.

Comparison of High School and College Play

The high school and college seasons usually start in the beginning of September, but the high school season ends eariler: most high schools play their last game in early November, and post-season competition begins the following week. Some state championships are conducted in one day while others last longer—the length of time varies from state to state. The same is true in determining which teams shall play in the tournament. Certain states invite all teams, several ask only the league champs, a number use combinations and many use a complicated point system to qualify, in which teams get a specific number of points during the season for wins and ties, and another amount when the teams they have beaten win their own games, the number depending on the ranking of the opponent. A few states have separate tournaments for public, private and parochial schools.

Tie-breaking rules vary from state to state as much as the norms for participating in post-season play. Some schools allow regular season games to remain as ties.

First, I will review the similarities between high school and college rules. The football field is marked the same in both. Two-point conversions are allowed after touchdowns and extra-point attempts are made from the 3-yard line. The free kick after a safety may be done with a tee. Teams have 25 seconds to get the ball in play,and the clock stops on every first down. There are no two-minute warnings.

A player is considered down if any part of his body other than his feet or hand touches the ground. Only one foot is required to be in bounds to complete a pass. Defensive pass interference results in a 15-yard penalty from the spot where the previous play was run. If the spot is inside the 30-yard line, the measurement is half the distance to the goal line.

Some major differences include game time. In college ball, there are four 15-minute quarters, while high school quarters are 12-minutes in duration. High schools have a mandatory three-minute warm-up at the end of halftime, shoes are required for kickers, and players must wear a mouth piece and tail bone pads. High schools kick off from the 40-yard line (colleges from the 35). High schools cannot score two-point *defensive* conversions (see Chapter 4), and most high schools have overtime rules while colleges do not. Many of these differences were instituted to insure the safety of players, for example, the shorter periods, mandatory warm-up, mouthpiece and extra padding.

19

Junior
Football

If your child plays football now—or soon will play in Little League, middle school or ninth grade—and you haven't learned the game, take the time to learn it now. Learning the game at this level is a piece of cake. There are fewer terms and play is simplified.

Little League, which usually includes children in the 10-to-13 age bracket, is the young athlete's first introduction to organized football. There are as many variations in leagues as there are communities sponsoring them, because each league makes its own by-laws. Most, however, use modified high school rules for play.

Safety First

Safety is the number one concern. There are relatively few serious injuries in little league play. My son said in two years of coaching in New Jersey he didn't have a single injury in practice or during a game (though one of his players broke his leg falling off a bike, and another sprained an ankle on his home basketball court).

Since head and neck injuries are the most serious kind, the players are required to wear a NOCSAE-approved helmet (see Chapter 12). The face mask must be one that offers maximum protection, and a participant may not play or practice without a cup and support and mouth guard. Shoulder pads are designed according to a player's weight. Teams are set up by weight as well as by age, in

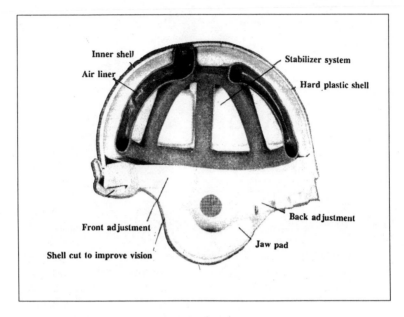

Illustration of a youth football helmet.

order to keep a 120-pound 10-year-old from tackling and falling on another 10-year-old who weighs 80 pounds.

Leagues furnish the necessary gear, like helmets, shoulder pads, jerseys, girdle pads and pants. In order to cover costs, there is a league entry fee, but no child is turned away because of financial reasons. The league absorbs the cost for these children.

Pop Warner Football

A typical league is the Pop Warner, named for Glenn Scobey Warner, one of America's greatest college football coaches, who coached for 47 years. Besides stressing the fundamentals of good football, academic achievement and community involvement are encouraged.

The league is divided into three divisions, **Pee Wee, Junior Midget** and **Midget. Pee Wee** players are ages ten and eleven and weigh no more than 100 pounds. Pee Wee games last for 20 clocked minutes, two 10 minute halves.

Junior Midget players are ages eleven and twelve, weigh no more than 115 pounds. Their games last for 32 minutes of playing time divided into 8 minute quarters.

Midget division games are played by twelve and thirteen year olds who weigh less than 135 pounds. **Midget** games last for 40 minutes divided into 10 minute quarters.

The Pop Warner league conducted its first annual national Super Bowl in 1987 with one game in each division.

There are 18 to 25 players per team, and coaches must play each one a minimum number of downs in a game. Three officials referee the game, and most will stop the game whenever necessary to explain to the players what they should or should not be doing. There are two weeks to a month of practice and conditioning prior to the start of the season, and then for 30-60 minutes before each game. During the season, one game and several practices take place each week. Since weight limits are strongly followed, an overweight player must either lose enough to play in his group or move up to the next weight level, where his weight will be comparable to that group.

Each level of play becomes more sophisticated because, as the players get older, they can comprehend more. The playing time becomes longer, the plays become more complex and new terms are added.

Junior High Competition

Middle school teams are made up of the largest 12- and 13- year-olds and those players in the seventh and eighth grades with the most dexterity and skill. The ones who do well here and like the game try out for ninth grade football, which serves as the bridge between Little League and high school competition.

20

Canadian Football

Canadian football is a fast-moving game with an emphasis on passing and kicking. Games last an average of 2½ hours, as compared to three or four hours in the NFL. If you haven't watched a Canadian game and have the opportunity, do so. You'll enjoy it.

Football has been played in Canada since 1865 and was patterned after English rugby where kicking and passing were stressed, but Canadian football grew from a two-game series in 1874 between McGill University and Harvard. In one game, Harvard rules were used: the ball could only be advanced by kicking (as in soccer); in the other, Canadian, rugby rules allowed running with the ball and throwing it. Football as we know it is a combination of both.

In earlier years, college and club teams made football popular, but it wasn't until the late 1950s (on the heels of the rise of the NFL) that professional football in Canada became well-established.

The Grey Cup

Lord Earl Grey, the Governor General of Canada, was a football enthusiast and thought there should be play for the Dominion championship. In 1909 he donated a trophy to be awarded for the Rugby Football Championship of Canada. This competition began the same year and three years later the trophy became known as the Grey Cup. Play included amateur and semipro teams as well as professional and the trophy could be challenged by any teams as long as the team was registered with the Canadian Rugby Union.

There were two pro leagues, Interprovincial Rugby Football Union (IRFU, known as Big Four) and Western Interprovincial Football Union (WIFU) which had five teams. In 1956 they joined to form the Canadian Football Council (CFC) and two years later broke away from the Canadian Rugby Union and changed their name to the Canadian Football League (CFL). Since 1954 only nine teams have challenged for the Grey Cup. Just prior to the 1987 season the Montreal Alouettes withdrew from the league. To balance the divisions, the Winnipeg team was moved to the Eastern Division.

The CFL Teams

Eastern Division
Hamilton Tiger-Cats
Ottawa Rough Riders
Toronto Argonauts
Winnipeg Blue Bombers

Western Division
B. C. Lions (Vancouver)
Calgary Stampeders
Edmonton Eskimos
Saskatchewan Roughriders

The CFL

The calendar year begins the third week in February when the CFL conducts an eight round college draft for non-import players. Like the NFL, the last place team in the league from the previous season gets first pick, the next to last team gets the second and so forth, with the Grey Cup winner from the previous year selecting last.

Training camp begins in mid-June. Each team plays two pre-season games. One team is selected to play in the annual Hall of Fame game at Hamilton against the Tiger-Cats during the regular season schedule.

The CFL (Canadian Football League) period of play extends from July through November, so a good part of the season overlaps the NFL and American college football seasons.

The two divisions, Eastern and Western, play an interlocking schedule. Each team plays an 18 game regular season schedule (half at home and half away) with every win counting two points and every tie, one.

The Grey Cup culminates the season the end of November. This is a game between the two divisions for the Canadian Football League championship. The three teams with the best won-lost-tied records in each division are in the playoffs. The second and third best record teams play in the first round and the winner plays the first place team for the division title and the right to be in the Grey Cup for the CFL championship.

CFL Awards

Besides the prestige of winning the Grey Cup there are numerous awards given for outstanding performances in the CFL, and many are to players on the championship team.

The CFL annually presents outstanding player awards. There are also 12 trophies, in addition to the one for the coach of the year, given for individual achievements.

The Football Reporters of Canada (FRC) select annual all-star teams: an All-Eastern, an All-Western and a CFL All-Star team.

As far as team awards, the Eastern Division winner receives the James S. Dixon Trophy and the Western is the recipient of the N. J. Taylor Trophy.

The CFL has broadened its interest in the game by becoming a founding partner in the International Football Federation (IFF) with Austria, Finland, France, Great Britain, Italy, The Netherlands, Switzerland and West Germany.

As you watch Canadian football you will see many variances, some major, but mostly minor, like terminology. I strongly recommend you get the latest Canadian *CFL Facts Figures & Records* rules book and learn the dissimilarities if you plan to watch with any regularity.

Differences Between NFL & CFL Rules

Following are the major differences in the CFL from the NFL:

1. The field is 110 yards long and 65 yards wide. Midfield is the 55-yard line.

2. 20 yards behind each goal line and parallel to it is the deadline. It is the same as the end line in the NFL.

3. The goal area, known as the end zone in the NFL, is

bounded by goal line, side-lines-in-goal and deadline.

4. Goal posts are centered on each goal line or if using a curved base, it must be set no further than 75 inches behind the goal line.

5. 36-man rosters: 14 Imports (players who have played football outside of Canada but not in Canada prior to their 17th birthdays), 20 non-imports (players who have lived 17 of their first 21 years in Canada and have never played football outside of Canada) and 2 quarterbacks, who may be imports. The number of roster players is reviewed annually.

6. Each team plays with 12 men on the field. The extra player, both on offense and defense, plays in the backfield.

7. There are seven eligible receivers on the offense, including the QB and the extra back.

8. There are no restrictions on the motion of offensive backs prior to the snap. They can move in any direction, including toward the line of scrimmage, provided they are not moving forward within one yard of the line of scrimmage at the snap.

9. The offense has three downs to gain 10 yards or give up possession of the ball.

10. The offense has 20 seconds to get the ball in play after the Referee's whistle signals time in.

11. A fumble may be legally advanced or kicked in any direction.

12. When a loose ball, other than a kick or incomplete pass, goes out of bounds, the team that last touched it in bounds retains possession.

13. The defensive players must line up at least one yard behind the line of scrimmage.

14. In place of the strong safety (SS) the defensive team has two "defensive halfbacks," one being the 12th man.

15. Three-minute warning before the end of each half.

16. Teams are not permitted timeouts except during the last three minutes of a half when each team is allowed one.

17. Overtime consists of two five-minute halves with two minutes in between. There is no sudden death. The entire time is played regardless of the amount of scoring during these 10 minutes. If the game is tied at the end of this time, it remains a tie unless it is a post season game when all play continues until the tie is broken.

18. There are six officials (no Side Judge).

19. The official ball for a CFL game is a Spalding J5V with two one-inch white stripes—one near each end.

20. Try-for-point(s) line of scrimmage is the 5-yard line.

21. There are no touchbacks. If a kick, other than an extra point attempt, is not returned out of the goal area, either in possession of a receiver, or if the ball touches or crosses the deadline or a side-line-in goal and touches the ground, a player, or some object beyond these lines, the kicking team is given one point called a "single" or "rouge."

22. After a score from a single the nonscoring team takes possession of the ball on its own 35-yard line. If the "single" was the result of a missed field goal attempt, the team scored against has the choice of placing the ball at either its own 35 or the line of scrimmage of the previous down.

23. A punt not touched by a member of the receiving team can be recovered by the punter or any teammate who was behind him when the ball was kicked. A punter in the CFL punts for field position more than hang time, and he can be blocked by an opponent in his attempt to get to the ball. after he has crossed the line of scrimmage.

24. There are no fair catches. Members of the kicking team must stay at least five yards away from the receiver until he touches or catches the ball.

25. After a field goal, the team scored against has another option other than kicking off or receiving a kickoff like in the NFL. It can choose possession of the ball at its own 35-yard line.

26. The yardage on successful field goals is measured from the point the ball is held to the *goal line*, where the goal post is located.

27. Two points may be scored after a touchdown by carrying or passing the ball across the goal line. Both one and two point attempts are called a "convert."

28. On a PAT attempt, the defense can advance a fumble, block the kick or intercept a pass and score two points (two-point convert return) by advancing the ball to the opposite end zone.

21

Football Etiquette

Just as there are rules of etiquette for dining and going to the theater, there are proper manners for a football game. As you read them, you'll see they really boil down to common sense and consideration.

Let's begin with the most important:

Don't be late. This is thoughtless anywhere, but especially so at a game. It's a cardinal rule and applies to the games on television as well as at a stadium. At home plan meals so everyone, including you, can see the kickoff.

Don't complain. This includes griping about the heat, cold, wind, snow, the climb to your seat or your seat location. After all, you are *there*. Many games are sellouts. The only thing you can complain about is your team losing. This is a sport and you should be a good one. Remember, everything about watching football should be fun.

Don't boo. The game is an outlet for the fans, a way to blow off steam, and it should be fun for them. Part of being a fan is not always agreeing with the coach's choice of play, an official's call of a foul, or a team's inept playing, but booing is poor sportsmanship, and that's a foul *you* should be penalized for.

What Not to Wear to a Game

Give careful thought to your wardrobe. It's one way to keep complaints to a minimum and enjoyment to a maximum. What should you wear? Depending on the weather I usually dress in two layers when I go to the Detroit Lions' games in the Pontiac Silverdome—one layer for the Michigan weather and the other for the comfortable 70's inside. There are diverse climate conditions around the country. You would dress differently for a December game in Chicago from one in Tampa Bay. It's important to know the latest weather prediction and dress accordingly.

Here are some things for ladies to consider in choosing what to wear:

- **No spike heels:** You want to keep up with the walking and don't want to fall on your face when you stand to cheer. Besides, no one has time to take you to the first aid station if you turn an ankle.
- **No delicate clothes:** Imagine what your silk dress or white slacks will look like when the hot dogs drip, your drink (or someone else's) spills, and the nachos melt. So hang it up and put on something comfortable. You're not going to a fashion show. A friend wore her mink coat to a Super Bowl in California and had beer spilled down her back. Now I ask you, was she there for show or comfort?
- **No odds and ends:** A shoulder bag is ideal for all the "things" a woman wants to have with her. But I found it's even better to wear a skirt with pockets so I don't need a purse. Just as sure as you have to retrieve a loose item like a scarf, the quarterback will throw a bomb and you'll miss seeing it.

Other Considerations

Now that you have an idea how to dress, let's talk about being considerate of those around you. If you're in a domed stadium, please don't smoke. Not only is it against the law in most places, but it violates non-smokers' rights. A couple of years ago, an experiment at the Pontiac Silverdome at half time showed the carbon monoxide level to be 15 times higher than safe industrial tolerance.

Try not to leave your seat any more than necessary. When you must leave, do so between plays, like a time-out, so you don't block the view of the game for all those people behind you.

You're attending because you're a fan, and at the stadium a fan should be self-reliant and uncomplaining—the kind who can handle whatever the weatherman and the fortunes of the game may bring. And do you know your reward? You'll be invited back again.

All of this proves the belief held by many veteran observers. The best sports, and the hardiest athletes, at a football game are the female fans.

22

Monday
Morning
Quarterbacking

NFL teams play 295 games a year. Count 'em: 283 regular and pre-season games (including Hall of Fame), 10 playoffs and the Super and Pro Bowls—plus even more if you count the American Bowl game played abroad. Obviously you can't see them all—even if you wanted to. Besides, that would be overkill. But just in case you feel deprived, don't fret. There are bonus nights on Mondays and occasional Thursdays and Sundays during the regular season. And they're free with a flick of the switch.

But maybe you didn't watch your team play on Sunday (horrors! How could you not?) or would like to know how another team fared. Hometown newspapers have several reporters covering their team, and you can read their articles in Monday's paper. Some are quite lengthy and detailed, so you might prefer just the highlights. The "NFL Summaries," "NFL Statistics" or a similar title depending on the newspaper, are for you. They recap each game in a limited amount of space—called box scores.

Let's look at the one for Superbowl XXIV, which took place in January, 1990:

Box score

San Francisco	13	14	14	14–55
Denver	3	0	7	0–10

FIRST QUARTER

San Francisco: Rice 20 pass from Montana (Cofer kick), 4:54. Drive: 66 yards, 10 plays. Key plays: Craig 18 run; Montana 9 pass to Rice; Montana 10 run. **San Francisco 7, Denver 0.** Denver: FG Treadwell 42, 8:13. Drive: 49 yards, 10 plays. Key plays: Elway 27 pass to Humphrey; Humphrey 10 run. **San Francisco 7, Denver 3.** San Francisco: Jones 7 pass from Montana (kick failed), 14:57. Drive: 54 yards, 10 plays. Key plays: Humphrey's fumble recovered by C.Brooks at San Francisco 46; Rathman 14 run; Montana 20 pass to Rice; Rathman 4 run on 4th and 1; Monatana 21 pass to Rice. **San Francis-**

co 13, Denver 3.

SECOND QUARTER

San Francisco: Rathman 1 run (Cofer kick), 7:45. Drive: 69 yards, 14 plays. Key plays: Montana 18 pass to Rathman; Craig 9 run; Montana 12 pass to Rathman; Montana 9 pass to Rathman; Rathman 1 run on 4th and 1. **San Francisco 20, Denver 3.**
San Francisco: Rice 38 pass from Montana (Cofer kick), 14:26. Drive: 59 yards, 5 plays. Key plays: Montana 9 pass to Walls. **San Francisco 27, Denver 3.**

THIRD QUARTER

San Francisco: Rice 28 pass from Montana (Cofer kick), 2:12. Drive: 28 yards, 1 play. Key play: Walter interception of Elway and 4 return. **San Francisco 34, Denver 3.**
San Francisco: Taylor 35 pass from Montana (Cofer kick), 5:16. Drive: 37 yards, 2 plays. Key play: C.Brooks interception of Elway and 38 return. **San Francisco 41, Denver 3.**
Denver: Elway 3 run (Treadwell kick), 8:07. Drive: 61 yards, 5 plays. Key plays: Elway 13 pass to Johnson; Humphrey 34 run. **San Francisco 41, Denver 10.**

FOURTH QUARTER

San Francisco: Rathman 4 run (Cofer kick), :03. Drive: 75 yards, 11 plays. Key plays: Craig 12 run; Rathman 18 run; Montana 12 pass to Rice; Montana 12 pass to Craig. **San Francisco 48, Denver 10.**
San Francisco: Craig 1 run (Cofer kick), 1:13. Drive: 1 yard, 1 play. Key play: Elway fumble recovered by Stubbs and 14 return to Denver 1. **San Francisco 55, Denver 10.**

TEAM STATISTICS

	S.F.	DEN.
First downs	28	12
Rushing	14	5
Passing	14	6
Penalty	0	1
Average gain-1st down	4.9	4.0
1st down passes	13	15
1st down pass avg. gain	7.43.1	
1st down rushes	20	8
1st down rush avg. gain	3.3	5.3
3rd-down efficiency	8-15	3-11
4th-down efficiency	2-2	0-0
Total plays	77	52
Total net yards	461	167
Average gain	6.0	3.2
Rushes-yards	44-144	17-64
Gain per rush	3.3	3.8
Passing yards	317	103
Completed-attempted	24-32	11-29
Net gain per pass	9.6	2.9
Had intercepted	0	2

Return yardage	129	207
Punts-returns	3-38	2-11
Kickoffs-returns	3-49	9-196
Interceptions	2-42	0-0
Fumbles-lost	0-0	3-2
Penalties-yards	4-38	0-0
Punts-average	4-39.5	6-38.5
Touchdowns	8	1
Rushing	3	1
Passing	5	0
Returns	0	0
Field goals	0-0	1-1
Time of possession	39:31	20:29

FIRST QUARTER

S.F.		DEN.
8	First downs	3
42	Net yards rushing	25
92	Net yards passing	27
7-12-0	Pass-Cmp.-Att.-Int.	1-7-0
3-5	3rd-down efficiency	1-3
10:36	Time of possession	4:24

SECOND QUARTER

S.F.		DEN.
8	First downs	2
38	Net yards rushing	-1
97	Net yards passing	37
8-9-0	Pass-Cmp.-Att.-Int.	5-13-0
2-4	3rd-down efficiency	0-3
10:19	Time of possession	4.41

THIRD QUARTER

S.F.		DEN.
7	First downs	5
38	Net yards rushing	41
109	Net yards passing	24
7-8-0	Pass-Cmp.-Att.-Int.	3-5-2
1-2	3rd-down efficiency	1-2
9:46	Time of possession	5:14

FOURTH QUARTER

S.F.		DEN.
5	First downs	2
26	Net yards rushing	-3
20	Net yards passing	51
2-3-0	Pass-Cmp.-Att.-Int.	3-5-0
2-4	3rd-down efficiency	1-3
8:50	Time of possession	6:10

The summaries appear the day following games, but the standings are published daily from pre-season through the Super Bowl. They break down the teams into each conference, then further into each of the three divisions, with the team having the best won-lost-tied record at the top of each division and the one with the worst at the bottom. An example which appeared in a major newspaper follows:

American Football Conference

EAST	W	L	T	PF	PA	H	A	NFC	AFC	DIV
x-Buffalo	9	7	0	409	317	6-2	3-5	1-3	8-4	6-2
Indianapolis	8	8	0	298	301	6-2	2-6	1-3	7-5	4-4
Miami	8	8	0	331	379	4-4	4-4	2-0	6-8	4-4
New Eng.	5	11	0	297	391	3-5	2-6	0-4	5-7	4-4
NY Jets	4	12	0	253	411	1-7	3-5	1-3	3-9	2-6

CENTRAL	W	L	T	PF	PA	H	A	NFC	AFC	DIV
x-Cleveland	9	6	1	334	254	*5-2	4-4	3-1	*6-5	3-3
y-Houston	9	7	0	365	412	6-2	3-5	3-1	6-6	3-2
Pittsburgh	9	7	0	265	326	4-4	5-3	3-1	6-6	1-5
Cincinnati	8	7	0	383	256	5-3	3-4	2-1	6-6	5-1

WEST	W	L	T	PF	PA	H	A	NFC	AFC	DIV
x-Denver	11	5	0	362	226	6-2	5-3	2-2	9-3	6-2
Kansas City	8	7	1	318	286	5-3	*3-4	2-0	*6-7	3-5
LA Raiders	8	8	0	315	297	7-1	1-7	2-2	6-6	3-5
Seattle	7	9	0	241	327	3-5	4-4	0-4	7-5	4-4
San Diego	6	10	0	266	290	4-4	2-6	2-2	4-8	4-4

* denotes a tie game
x clinched division title; y clinched wild-card playoff berth

National Football Conference

CENTRAL	W	L	T	PF	PA	H	A	NFC	AFC	DIV
Green Bay	10	6	0	362	356	6-2	4-4	10-4	0-2	5-3
Minnesota	9	6	0	322	254	7-0	2-6	8-4	1-2	6-2
Detroit	7	9	0	312	364	4-4	3-5	6-6	1-3	4-4
Chicago	6	10	0	358	377	4-4	2-6	4-8	2-2	2-6
Tampa Bay	5	11	0	320	419	2-6	3-5	5-7	0-4	3-5

EAST	W	L	T	PF	PA	H	A	NFC	AFC	DIV
x-NY Giants	12	4	0	348	252	7-1	5-3	8-4	4-0	6-2
y-Phila.	11	5	0	342	274	6-2	5-3	8-4	3-1	7-1
Washington	10	6	0	386	308	4-4	6-2	8-4	2-2	4-4
Phoenix	5	11	0	258	377	2-6	3-5	4-8	1-3	2-6
Dallas	1	15	0	204	393	0-8	1-7	1-13	0-2	1-7

WEST	W	L	T	PF	PA	H	A	NFC	AFC	DIV
x-San Fran.	14	2	0	442	253	6-2	8-0	10-2	4-0	5-1
y-LA Rams	11	5	0	426	344	6-2	5-3	8-4	3-1	4-2
New Orleans	9	7	0	386	301	5-3	4-4	5-7	4-0	3-3
Atlanta	3	13	0	279	437	3-5	0-8	1-11	2-2	0-6

Glossary

alignment—The way the defense lines up to oppose the offense before the ball is centered. The player in charge of the defensive huddle usually calls which "alignment" will be used.

audible (audiblize)—A quick change of plans decided by the quarterback at the line of scrimmage. He makes a switch in the play from the one he had just announced in the team huddle by calling a different set of signals. Also called "automatic" and "check off."

backfield, defensive—defensive backs—cornerbacks and safeties—collectively known as defensive backfield and "secondary."

backfield, offensive backs—players who line up behind the line of scrimmage—collectively known as the offensive backfield.

balanced formation—When a formation includes a receiver or receivers on one side of the ball equal to blocking help and running back(s) on the other.

blind-side a player—Hit a player from back or side without him seeing the block or tackle coming.

blitz—A sudden rush on the quarterback by linebackers and/or secondary, to stop a pass. When only linebackers rush to stop the pass as well as the run, it's known as a "red dog."

blitz out of the dime—A pass rush by the secondary when there are six defensive backs.

blitz out of the nickel—A pass-rush by the secondary when there are five defensive backs.

block—To bodily obstruct by using any portion of the body above the knees to make contact with an opponent.

bomb—A long pass.

bootleg—The quarterback fakes a handoff to a running back, hides the ball against his hip and either runs with it around the end, pitches it out to another back or passes it.

boxman—An official responsible for the down indicator that shows the current down and marks the ball location at the start of each down.

break a tackle—Ball carrier is hit by a defender but avoids being tackled.

break formation—Use unusual offensive formations like three wide receivers instead of the usual one or two.

break the plane—Enter the vertical plane of the neutral zone, end zone or the receiving team's restraining line.

break up a pass—Knock the ball down before an offensive player catches it.

broken field running—An offensive ball carrier's gain through the defense, where there are no blockers or where the ball carrier sets up the defensive players so the blockers can knock the defensive players down.

broken play—An offensive play made when the original plan becomes impossible, either because the defense anticipated the play or an offensive player failed in his assignment.

brush block—An offensive quick light block to slow down a defensive player.

bullet pass—A pass thrown hard.

bump—See "chuck."

burned—A defensive player does not carry out his assignment and his man makes a long run or catches a pass.

cadence—The series of numbers, words or phrases the quarterback calls at the line of scrimmage just prior to the start of each play.

center (offensive player)—The middle interior lineman who snaps or centers the ball to begin every offensive play.

center the ball—To hike, hand back, pass back or snap the ball to begin a play. This is done by handing or throwing the ball through the center's legs to the quarterback or whoever is to receive it.

chain gang (crew)—The seven assistant officials who handle the yardage chain along the sidelines.

change field—Between the first and second and third and fourth quarters the teams reverse ends of the field. They change goals to defend. The ball is put in play at a point corresponding exactly to the point at the other end of the field where the ball became dead at the end of the previous quarter and in exactly the same way as if play had not been stopped.

check off—See "audible."

chuck—The defense is allowed to give an eligible receiver one block, shove or push within five yards of the line of scrimmage. Also called "jam."

claim on waiver—To sign a player who has been unconditionally released by another team.

clip—To block a player who does not have the ball by either hitting him below the waist while moving up from behind or throwing the body across the back of his leg(s), unless the action is in close to the line of scrimmage.

cock—To raise or draw back, such as when the quarterback "cocks" his arm before passing the ball.

coffin corner—The area on the field close to the intersection of a sideline and the opposing team's goal line.

contain defense—To play conservatively and allow only short yardage on runs and passes.

contained play—The ball carrier is forced toward the center of the field and away from a sideline.

conversion—The point(s) scored after a touchdown by a kick, pass or run. Also a first down earned on third down by having advanced the ball the necessary 10 yards.

cornerbacks—The defensive backs who line up closest to the sidelines.

count—See "cadence."

crackback block—A legal block by a wide receiver within five yards of the line of scrimmage so long as the opponent is not hit from behind or below the waist.

crawling—Illegal attempt by the ball carrier to advance after he has been tackled.

curl—A pass pattern in which the receiver runs downfield and then curls back toward the line of scrimmage.

cut—To change direction.

cutback—An offensive move by the ball carrier when he swerves suddenly and goes diagonally to the other side.

dead ball—A ball no longer in play.

dead ball foul—A rule violation after a down ends.

deep man—A punt receiver, a pass receiver, or a defensive back.

defense—The team not having possession of the ball.

defensive backfield—See "secondary."

defensive ends—The down linemen on the outside of each tackle in a 4-3 defensive alignment or on each side of the nose tackle—also called nose and middle guard—in a 3-4 alignment.

defensive tackle—One of the two down linemen between the ends in a 4-3 defensive alignment. In a 3-4, one lines up between the ends and is called either a nose tackle, nose guard or middle guard.

delay of game—A team's failure to be ready within the appropriate limit. Any action that intentionally lengthens the game.

depth chart—A graph showing the names of the players used to play each position.

dime back—The sixth man in the defensive secondary. Since there are usually four, the fifth is a nickel and the sixth is a dime.

dime defense—A defensive alignment with six defensive backs.

dog—A defensive maneuver by one or more linebackers to confuse the offense by giving up the usual rushing route for a different path. When linemen "dog," it is known as a "stunt." **double coverage**—Two defenders covering one offensive player on a pass play. **double-foul**—A violation by each team on the same down.

double-team—Two players on one team assigned to one player on the other team.

double-team block—Two offensive players, usually linemen, blocking one defender.

down—The period of action that begins when the ball is centered or free-kicked and ends when it's whistled dead.

down—When any part of the body, other than the feet or hands of the player in possession of the ball, touches the ground, the player is "down" and all game action stops.

downfield—the scoring direction of the team with the ball.

down indicator (marker)—A four feet high pole topped with four numbered flip cards—1, 2, 3 and 4. The cards indicate the current down and the pole is located along the sidelines, marking the ball location at the start of each down.

down linemen—The defensive players who line up in a three- or four-point stance at the line of scrimmage opposite the offensive team's interior linemen.

down the ball—To stop play intentionally by touching one knee to the ground while having possession of the ball or by touching the ball anywhere on the field when doing so makes the ball dead, like by a member of the kicking team following a punt.

draft—The formal procedure of a fixed number of rounds each year where pro teams pick players from the college ranks.

draft choice—A player who has completed his college eligibility and has been selected by a pro club. The team that "drafts" him has the exclusive right to sign him to a contract. No other team in the league can bid for his service.

draw play—The quarterback steps back as though to pass, thus drawing in the defensive linemen. Then he either keeps the ball or hands it off to another back who runs through the gap left by the on-charging defenders. Also called "mousetrap."

drive start—Sideline pole marker that indicates the origin of a team's ball possession, which is moved only when the ball possession changes.

drop back—As soon as the QB receives the ball from the center on a passing play he retreats about seven yards before throwing it.

dropkick—Seldom used kick in which the kicker intentionally drops the ball on the ground and kicks it immediately after it hits the ground.

dual possession—See "simultaneous catch or possession."

elephant line—The heaviest offensive linemen. They are used for short yardage.

eligible receivers—The players who can legally catch passes. On the offensive team they are the two ends on the scrimmage line and the players in the backfield who are at least one yard behind the line of scrimmage. The QB is eligible only in the shotgun formation. All the offensive players become eligible after the ball touches an eligible receiver or a defensive player. All players on the defensive team are always eligible to intercept a pass.

encroachment—A defensive player may enter the neutral zone and retreat without a penalty before the ball is centered but is guilty of encroachment if he draws an opponent offside or makes contact with an opponent.

end—See "defensive end" and "offensive end."

end around—An offensive play where a tight end or wide receiver circles back behind the quarterback for a lateral or handoff.

end lines—The two boundaries on a football field that are 10 yards beyond the goal lines.

end zone—The area at each end of the football field from the goal line to the end line.

even defense—An even number of down linemen. See "four-three."

exhibition game—One whose result has no effect on the official standings of the teams and records of the players.

fade back—See "drop back."

fair catch—The signal made by a player who is about to receive a punt, kickoff or safety kick. He fully extends one arm above his head and waves it from side to side while the ball is in flight. This indicates he will not attempt to run with the ball after he catches it. Once he makes this signal he must be allowed to catch the ball and cannot be tackled by any member of the kicking team.

fair catch kick—Following a fair catch, the receiving team may try an uncontested field goal from the yard line of the catch. No tee may be used and the opposing team must line up at least 10 yards downfield from the ball just like a kickoff.

fake reverse—Ball carrier pretends to handoff to a teammate running laterally in the opposite direction.

false start—When an offensive lineman breaks his three-point stance or any offensive player, other than the man in motion, simulates the start of a down before the ball is centered.

field goal—A three point play scored by the offensive team's placekicking (or dropkicking) the ball from scrimmage above the opposing team's crossbar and between the uprights of the goal post.

field position—The spot on the field where the offensive team begins its next play. How good or poor a team's position is determined by the location of the ball in relation to the defensive goal line.

first round—The first round in a predetermined number (at present it is 12) for NFL teams to select college players. Since there are 28 teams there are normally 28 first- round draft selections.

flag on the play—An official throws his flag to indicate a foul has been committed. This "flag" or penalty marker is a weighted yellow handkerchief that he throws on the field at or near the spot of the infraction.

flanker (flankerback)—An offensive player, also known as a wide receiver, who usually lines up on the same side of a formation as the tight end and about a yard behind the line of scrimmage. However, he may line up on the split end side or with the running backs.

flare pass—A pass thrown to a running back who is near the line of scrimmage and takes off in a horizontal direction for the nearer sideline. Also "swing pass."

flat—The area of the field just beyond the line of scrimmage and next to the sidelines.

flea flicker—A deceptive offensive play designed to make the defense think it's going to be a running play. The quarterback hands the ball off to a back who laterals or pitches back to the quarterback who then passes the ball.

flood a zone—Offense sends more than one receiver into a specific area.

fly pattern—The straight downfield pass route the wide receivers run.

force a play—To make the runner commit himself to a specific direction.

force defense—Defense uses aggressive tactics such as "stunts" and "dogs" against the running game and "blitzing" and "man-for-man" receiver coverage against the passing game.

formation—Technically a formation is any arrangement, but in football to distinguish the way the two teams assemble at the line to start a play, the words "formation," "offensive formation" and "set" are used for the offense and the word "alignment" for defense.

forward pass—A ball thrown toward the opponent's goal line.

forward stake indicator—Fluorescent vinyl arrow placed on the ground along the sidelines opposite the yardage chains, which shows the distance necessary for getting a first down.

foul—An infraction of the game rules, subject to a

yardage penalty.

four (4) down line—See "front four."

four-point stance—Two hands on the ground when lining up at the scrimmage line.

four-three (4-3), (4-3-4) or (43)—Defensive alignment with four down linemen, three linebackers and four defensive backs (secondary).

free agent—An eligible collegiate player who has not been drafted by the NFL or a pro player who has been unconditionally released and no team in the league claims him. He is free to negotiate and sign a contract with any team wanting him.

free ball—A loose live ball.

free kick—A kick—whether a kickoff, following a safety or after a fair catch—in which the opposing team cannot interfere with the kicker because they must be lined up no closer than 10 yards from the kicking team's line.

free kick down—a kick that starts with a free kick.

free safety—The defensive backfield player between the cornerbacks who usually lines up on the opposite side of the ball from the offensive team's tight end, but is free to roam.

front four—The four down linemen in a 4-3 defensive alignment. They make up the front line.

front line—The players who line up at the line of scrimmage—both offense and defense.

front three—The three down linemen in a 3-4 defensive alignment.

fullback—An offensive backfield player who is usually the largest and strongest of the running backs.

fumble—To unintentionally drop the ball in one's

possession before being tackled or out of bounds.

game plan—A plan of action designed by the head coach and his assistants and used in practice prior to each game.

general manager—The team executive who directs the day-to-day team operations, including player trades and contracts.

give—A handoff of the ball.

goal line—One of the two lines the width of the playing field that separates the 100-yard field of play from the end zone.

goalpost—The structure at each end of the playing field made up of two uprights, a crossbar and a padded curved base.

go route—See "fly pattern."

go to the post—A pass pattern where the receiver runs downfield and then angles toward the goal post.

gridiron—The football field.

grounding—Drop to one knee with the ball. See "intentional grounding."

ground game—Running plays.

Hail Mary—A long high pass thrown in desperation, usually at the end of a half or game, into the end zone, hoping an offensive player will catch it or be interfered with.

half (halftime)—The 12 minute intermission between the second and third quarters when the teams leave the field and go to their respective locker rooms.

halfback—An offensive backfield player who is usually the fastest and lightest of the running backs.

handkerchief—See "flag on the play."

handoff—The handing of the ball from one teammate to another.

hang time—The amount of time a ball stays in the air after a punt or kickoff.

hashmarks—The two short lines intersecting each five yard line 23 yards, 1-3/4 feet (70' 9") in from the sidelines.

hike—See "center the ball."

hit—An attempted tackle. Also forceful contact between players.

hitman—Defensive player assigned to cover the quarterback.

home-field advantage—The mental lift from home town crowds tends to make teams win more games at home than away.

hook pass pattern—A delay route used by the tight end to fool the defense. He makes a few short forward zigzags and then runs in a hook-like direction back toward the middle of the field.

huddle—Usually before each down the offensive players gather in a group or circle behind the line of scrimmage for the QB to tell them the next play and the signals he'll be calling. The defensive team may form a loose huddle on its side of the line for the captain to announce the next alignment.

hurry-up offense—Used to get the most plays out of the least amount of time. Several consecutive ones are decided in one huddle.

illegal motion—More than one offensive backfield man moving, or the man in motion moving in a forward direction, during the final second before the ball is snapped.

incomplete pass—A pass not caught before touching the ground.

ineligible receiver—Interior offensive linemen and the QB, except in the Shotgun formation, until the ball is touched by an eligible receiver. Then they all become eligible.

injured reserve list—While players are recuperating their names are placed on an official list and temporarily removed from the team's roster.

inside running play—A running play between the two offensive tackles.

intentional grounding—Ball passer deliberately throws the ball to the ground or out of bounds so he won't be tackled for a loss of yardage.

interception—A pass intended for an offensive receiver is caught by a defensive player in bounds before it touches the ground.

interference—1. Fair-catch interference—When a fair catch is called, no kicking team member may interfere with the receiver, the ball or the receiver's path to the ball. 2. Run Interference—It is legal for an offensive player to protect the ball carrier by lawfully blocking opposing players. 3. Pass Interference—It is illegal to hinder either a receiver's (offense) or defender's (defense) attempt to reach a pass or wave the hands so he can't see the ball.

interior line—The five offensive inside linemen: the center, two guards and two tackles.

interior lineman—One of the five linemen making up the "interior line."

in the grasp—To seize and hold the quarterback long enough for an official to blow the play dead. This is equivalent to being tackled.

jam—See "chuck."

juke—A move by a ball carrier or pass receiver to escape a defender.

jumbo or heavy jumbo—See "elephant line."

keeper—QB keeps the ball and dives forward for short yardage.

key in on a play—To look for or find a clue as to what the offensive play is going to be.

key on a player—to watch one offensive player.

key on the ball—To watch the center's hand and football to anticipate when the ball will be snapped.

kick from scrimmage—A punt or field goal attempt.

kickoff—The method used to put the ball into play, from an artificial kicking tee or held by a teammate, to start the game and the second half, after a field goal, following an extra point try after a touchdown and to begin overtime play. The ball is kicked from the kicking team's 35-yard line, (unless an infraction preceded the kick) and the opposing team must line up at least 10 yards downfield from the ball.

lateral pass—Any pass other than a forward one. It can be backward or parallel to the line of scrimage.

lead block—To run along just ahead of the runner and keep away would-be tacklers.

linebacker—One of three or four defensive players who line up behind or between the down linemen, usually in an upright position.

line of scrimmage—As the ball rests on the field to begin the next play, it is the imaginary line for each team at the point of the ball nearer its goal line and runs across the field from sideline to sideline. After the ball is snapped, there is one line of scrimmage where the forward point of the ball was.

line up—To take a position at one's line of scrimmage, before a down begins.

live ball—Ball in play from the time a down begins until the down ends.

look off—QB looks in one direction and passes in the opposite.

loose ball—A live ball not in any player's possesion during game action.

lose ground—Lose yardage.

make the play—Successful completion of a plan.

man-for-man defense—Each pass defender is assigned a specific receiver to cover.

man-in-motion—An offensive backfield player who moves during the final second before the ball is snapped. His movement is limited to a parallel or retreating direction from the line of scrimmmage.

man-to-man—See man-for-man.

marker—Symbol officials use to indicate important field locations like the spot of a fumble during a play.

middle guard—Same as "nose guard."

misdirected play—The offense tricks the defense into committing itself to going in one direction while the ball carrier runs in the other.

monster man—A fifth linebacker in a 3-4 defensive alignment. He can change between being a linebacker or secondary man.

mousetrap—See "draw play."

muff—The touching or accidental kicking of a loose ball by a player in an unsuccessful attempt to gain possession of it.

multiple foul—Two or more infractions by a team on the same play.

net points—The total points a team scores during a season minus the total number it has given up to its opponents.

neutral zone—The territory between the offensive and defensive lines of scrimmage which runs across the field from sideline to sideline.

nickel back—The fifth man in the secondary. Since there are usually four, the extra (or 5th one) is the nickel back.

nickel defense—A defensive alignment with five defensive backs.

no huddle offense—See "hurry-up offense."

nose guard—A defensive down lineman who lines up in an alignment nose to nose with the offensive team's center.

nose tackle—Another name for the nose guard.

odd defense—An odd number of down linemen.

offense—The team in legal possession of the ball.

offensive end—One of the two offensive linemen who are eligible receivers. He lines up on the outside of a tackle either some distance away (split end) or close (tight end).

offensive formation—The order in which the offensive players line up before the ball is centered. Also called "set."

offensive guard—One of the two offensive linemen who line up on each side of the center.

offensive line—The seven players at the line of scrimmage when the ball is centered.

offensive lineman—One of the seven players on the offensive line.

offensive tackle—One of the two offensive linemen who

line up next to and outside the guards.

official (assistant)—One positioned along the sidelines with a specific duty.

official (field)—One of a seven-man crew employed by the NFL to officiate on the field. He wears a black and white striped shirt, has specific responsibilities and enforces the rules of the game.

official (replay)—Person employed by the NFL to sit in a booth above the field and check specific calls made by the field officials.

offsetting fouls—A violation by each team on the same play so both penalties are nullified and the down is played over from the same spot.

offside—A violation when any part of a player's body is beyond his scrimmage or free kick line when the ball is snapped or kicked.

off-tackle running play—Ball carrier heads outside one of the tackles.

one-on-one—One offensive player competing against one defensive player.

onside kick—A kickoff intended to go only the required 10 yards so the kicking team can try to recover it.

on the sidelines—Out of bounds anywhere along either of the 120 yard sides of the playing field.

open field running—See "broken field running."

open set—See "pro set."

operate out of the spread—Use a formation with the wide receivers positioned near the sidelines.

option—Ball carrier has a planned choice of doing one of several things.

option running—Find the best hole and run through it.

out of bounds—On or outside the sidelines and end lines.

outside run—Ball carrier runs toward one of the sidelines.

overload a zone—See "flood a zone."

overtime—If the score is tied at the end of regulation play, the game continues after a three-minute intermission until one team scores or until 15 minutes of playing time elapses. If neither scores, the game ends in a tie except in post-season playoff games when overtime periods continue until one team scores to break the tie. The first overtime begins with a coin toss and kickoff, succeeding periods are treated the same as changing goals between the first and second quarters in a regulation game.

own goal—The goal a team is defending, the one behind it as it lines up at the scrimmage line.

pass—To throw the football from one player to another.

pass action play—QB looks like he's dropping back to pass, then hands off the ball or throws a short pass behind the scrimmage line.

pass back—See "center the ball."

pass coverage—To cover all possible pass receivers.

pass rush—Quick defensive pressure on the QB when a pass is suspected, to either sack him, cause him to throw the ball prematurely, or better yet, fumble.

PAT—Point After Touchdown.

pattern—Predesignated route of a pass receiver.

penalty—Punishment imposed for breaking a rule.

period (quarter)—15 minutes of official playing time.

personal foul—An individual player's being unnecessarily rough against an opposing player.

pick off—To intercept a pass.

pick up yardage—To gain distance and move closer to opponent's goal line.

pigskin—The football. A misconceived term because a football is made from cowhide.

pitch-out—A short underhand lateral toss of the ball.

pits—See "trenches."

placekick—To kick the ball from a fixed position on the ground. A team mate may hold the ball. An artificial kicking tee may be used on the kickoff.

place-kicker—A player who specializes in kickoffs and/or field goals and/or extra point attempts.

platoon—To use one squad of players for offense and another for defense.

play—The offensive team's plan for the next down and the down itself.

play action pass—(play-fake pass) QB fakes a handoff and then drops back to pass.

playbook—A team's manual detailing all the plays a team uses.

play out contract—To perform all obligations in a written contract.

pocket—The protected area behind the line of scrimmage the offensive blockers form around the QB on a passing play.

pooch—A short high punt.

possession—Legal control of ball.

post pattern—See "go to the post."

post-possession foul—Infraction following change of possession of the ball after a punt.

power play—A running play with considerable blocking help.

prevent defense—The defensive team plays loose and deep, often with five or six men in the backfield. It will concede a short gain but guards against a long pass.

primary receiver—The first choice receiver in a passing play.

pro bowler—A player who has played in a Pro Bowl game held each year the week after the Super Bowl.

pro set—Most commonly used offensive formation.

pull—An interior lineman runs laterally from his position at the snap to block either side.

pump fake—To draw back the throwing arm with the ball as if to pass, but not throw the ball.

punt—To drop the ball and kick it, before it hits the ground.

punter—A player who specializes in punting.

pylon—Flexible vinyl markers at the inside corners of the four intersections of the goal lines and sidelines and at each corner of the end lines.

quarter—See "period."

quarterback—The offensive captian who lines up immediately behind the the center, except in the shotgun formation. He calls the plays and receives the ball directly from the center, except on kicking plays.

quarterback rating system—The NFL grades QBs on their performance. Points are given for average passing gain and the percentage of passes completed, those resulting in touchdowns and those intercepted.

quarterback sneak—See "keeper."

quick kick—Punt on any down prior to the fourth.

quick opener—Instead of waiting for his blockers the ball carrier runs through the interior line as fast as he can.

read a play—To predict what a particular play will be.

read the defense or offense—To predict what the other team will do.

recover—Regain possession of the ball after a fumble.

red dog—A sudden rush on the QB by one or more linebackers to stop the run as well as the pass. When either linebackers and/or the defensive backs are used to stop a pass, it's a "blitz."

referee—The head official who, among his duties, indicates, interprets and announces the infractions and penalties.

reserve—A player who is not immediately available to play with a team.

return-kick—A kick made by a player immediately after catching a kick.

reverse—The ball carrier heads toward a sideline and then hands off the ball in the backfield to a runner going in the opposite direction.

rodman—One of two assistant officials who tends the yardage chains. See "yardage chain."

roll out—Instead of dropping back in the pocket on a passing play, the QB runs to his right or left while looking for a receiver.

rookie—First year pro player.

roster—List of all the players on a team eligible to play in each regular season and postseason game.

round—A complete cycle whereby each NFL team picks one unchosen college player in the "draft."

rover—See "free safety."

runner—A player carrying the ball.

running back—An offensive player, other than the QB or wide receiver, who lines up at least one yard behind the line of scrimmage. Includes fullback, halfback, setback, slotback, tailback and wing back.

sack—Tackle the QB behind the line of scrimmage before he releases the ball.

safety (player)—A defensive backfield man who lines up between cornerbacks.

safety (score)—The only way the defense can score points without getting possession of the ball. It is awarded two points and receives the kickoff from its opponents 20-yard line, if the ball carrier is tackled in his end zone, or the ball is otherwise blown dead on or behind the offensive team's goal line.

safety blitz—A sudden rush on the quarterback by a safety, one of the defensive backfield players.

safety kick—Following a safety (score) the team scored upon free kicks from its own 20-yard line with no tee.

safety-valve pass—A pass to a player near the line of scrimmage when the downfield receivers are covered.

scoreboard—A large stadium board that gives relative information during a game. It shows the names of the teams, the score, quarter, time remaining in the quarter, the down, yards to go for a first down, timeouts and the team with the ball.

scout—A team representative who researches college players, collects information and films, and charts future NFL opponents.

screen pass—The defensive linemen are allowed to come through the offensive line and the QB floats the ball over their heads.

scrimmage—Practice football game. See "line of scrimmage."

scrimmage down—A down that starts with a snap, like a running play, as opposed to a free kick down that starts with a free kick, like a kickoff. It is most often called simply a down. See "down."

seams—The part of the field where two defensive zones overlap.

second and long (or short)—Second down and long (or short) yardage to go for a first down.

secondary—Defensive backfield. The defensive backs include the cornerbacks and safeties.

second clock—Clock used to time the 45 or 30 seconds allowed between downs. There are identical clocks at each end of the field and they are visibly located for the players, officials and fans to see.

second effort—Added attempt by a runner to gain more yardage after it appears the defense has stopped his forward progress.

set—Offensive team arrangement. See "formation" and "offensive formation."

set—See "set position."

set a pick—Use a player or official to screen a defensive player from an intended receiver.

setback—The lone running back in a formation.

set position—Complete stop. Stationary.

shift—Movement by two or more offensive backfield players at the same time up to one second before the snap.

short side of the field—The side of the field from where the ball is spotted that has less area to the sideline than on the other side of the ball.

shotgun—Offensive formation. The only one where the QB receives the centered ball five yards back and is an eligible receiver.

shovel pass—A short forward pass to a receiver behind the line of scrimmage.

signals—Prearranged number, word, color or phrase the QB will call when the ball is to be snapped to start a play.

simultaneous catch or possession—Unusual situation where an offensive and a defensive player gain possession of the ball at the same time, like in a pass reception. The ball is awarded to the offense.

slant pattern—From his position, a wide receiver runs out in a slanting angle to the place on the field where the pass is to be thrown.

slotback—A running back who lines up in the area between the split end and the tackle, a yard behind the line.

snap—See "center the ball."

snapper—The player (center) who snaps the ball to start a scrimmage down.

spear—To butt with the crown of the helmet.

special teams—Players used in kicking situations.

spiral (football)—Spin on its longer axis.

split end—An offensive lineman who lines up on the line a few yards (split) outside the nearer tackle and is an eligible receiver. Also called "wide receiver."

spot the ball—Place the ball on "the spot" or the hashmark on the field where the next play is to begin.

spy—A defensive player on the line watches for a fake play, such as a running or passing play, when a field goal attempt is expected.

starting players—First string.

Statue of Liberty—Offensive play. The QB receives the ball from center, drops back and cocks his arm as if to pass while a teammate, usually a running back, runs behind him and takes the ball out of his hand.

stiff-arm (straight-arm)—To push away a tackler with a straight arm. Only the ball carrier may use his hands to keep away would-be tacklers.

streak pass route—See "fly pattern."

strike—To make contact with an opponent by swinging, clubbing, or propelling either the arm or forearm.

stripes—The five-yard lines.

strip the ball—To tear away the ball from the runner before or during a tackle.

strong safety—The defensive backfield player between the cornerbacks who lines up on the same side of the ball as the offensive team's tight end.

strong side—The side of the ball on which the tight end (TE) lines up.

stunt—A defensive linemen trick to confuse the offense. They change their usual straight ahead rushing and go a different route. When linebackers do it, it's called a "dog."

sudden death—The first team to score in overtime wins, whether by TD, FG or safety.

sweep—When ball carrier runs between the tight end and the sideline.

swing—The horizontal route a ball carrier runs when he heads for the nearer sideline. **swing pass**—See "flare pass."

tackle—To pull or knock down the ball carrier so any part of his body other than his feet or hands touches the ground.

tackle (player)—See "defensive tackle" and "offensive tackle."

tailback—Offensive backfield player. One of the running backs whose position in a formation is farthest back from the line of scrimmage as in the I formation.

third and short (or long)—Third down and short (or long) yardage for a first down.

three (3) down linemen—See "front three."

three-four (3-4), (3-4-4) or (34)—Defensive alignment. The first number gives the number of players on the line. The second shows how many are in the middle and the third gives the number in the backfield.

three-point stance—One hand on the ground when lining up at the line of scrimmage.

throw away—To intentionally throw the ball out of bounds for an incomplete pass.

tight end—Offensive lineman who lines up outside (tight to) a tackle.

time out—The period of time in a game when play is halted and the official clock is stopped.

time the hit—To tackle the pass receiver the instant he

catches the ball, hoping to jar the ball loose.

touchback—There is no score or penalty to receive a kickoff or punt in one's own end zone and remain there with the ball without advancing beyond the goal line. In other words, not stepping into the playing field. It's also a touchback on a kickoff or punt if the ball enters the receiving team's end zone and then goes out of bounds. When a defender intercepts a pass in his own zone, it is likewise a touchback. The ball is ruled dead in possession of the receiving team, placed on its 20-yard line, and now the receiving team becomes the offense.

touchdown—The six points awarded to a team when the ball is legally in possession of one of its in-bounds players when any part of the ball is over, on or above the opponent's goal line.

training camp—Preseason player practice and tryouts.

trap block—After the snap a defensive lineman is allowed to advance while an offensive lineman comes from an unexpected direction and blocks the defender from the side.

trap play—A play with a trap block.

trap the ball—Entrap a ball between the ground and hands. It is not legally caught since it has touched the ground prior to being possessed.

trenches—Area near the scrimmage line where the linemen, both the down (defense) and interior (offense), meet in combat.

triple action—Either the quarterback, halfback or fullback carries the ball, depending on what the strong side of the defense does.

try-for-point—Also "try" and "PAT." Extra-point attempt after a touchdown.

turn over—Offensive team loses possession of the ball through a fumble or intercepted pass.

turn the ball over—See "turn over."

two-minute drill—See "hurry-up offense."

two-minute offense—See "hurry-up offense."

two minute warning— Referee notifies each head coach when approximately two minutes are left to play in each half. There is no two-minute warning in overtime.

two-point stance—An upright position, as opposed to a crouched three (one hand on the ground) or four-point (both hands on the ground) stance.

unanswered points—Consecutive points scored by one team with none scored from the other team.

unbalanced formation—Opposite of balanced formation. Receivers on one side of the ball are not balanced by blockers and ball carrier on the other.

unconditional release—Free from a contract with no restrictions.

unsportsmanlike conduct—A player's, team's or coach's behavior an official deems contrary to good sportsmanship. A non-contact foul.

upfield—Synonymous with downfield.

uprights—The two vertical posts on a goal post that rise 30 feet above the crossbar.

veteran—A player with at least one year of professional playing experience.

waiver(s)—Contract of a player to be released is offered to the other teams at his present salary.

wave off—See "look off."

weak safety—See "free safety."

weak side—The side of the ball where the split end (SE)

lines up.

wideout—A wide receiver.

wide receiver—An offensive player who is an eligible receiver (see "eligible receiver") and lines up wide of a tight end or tackle either at or near the line of scrimmage, like a split end or a flanker.

wide side of the field—The side of the field where the ball is spotted that has more area to the sideline than on the other side of the ball.

wing back—A running back who lines up close behind but just to the outside of a tight end.

wishbone—Offensive formation with the backfield men lined up ressembling a chicken wishbone.

work the clock—To use the clock (time) to one's advantage, such as taking time-outs, throwing the ball out of bounds or using the hurry-up offense.

X pole (drive start)—Sideline marker that shows where a team's ball possession originated and is moved only when ball possession changes. It is tended by an assisstant official.

yardage chain—A 10 yard length of chain connected by a five foot high rod at either end. The chain is used to determine if the offensive team has gained at least 10 yards in four downs or fewer, and is tended along the sidelines by two assistant officials (rodmen).

zone blocking—Blocking any defensive player(s), who comes into a specific area of the field.

zone defense—A type of defense in which each pass defender is responsible for a specific area of the field.